# which
# wine
# when

# which wine when

What to drink with the food you love

*by* Bert Blaize & Claire Strickett

EBURY
PRESS

*For all the friends who've ever*
*asked us what to drink.*

# CONTENTS

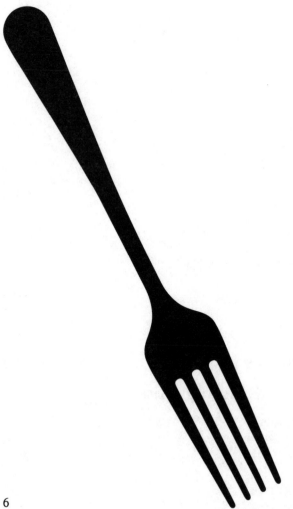

# INTRODUCTION

This is a book for everyone who finds themselves struggling over and over again to pick a bottle of wine to drink with dinner based on anything more than a pretty label, a special offer or a vague memory.

The recommendations here will give you the knowledge and confidence you need to decide which wine will be the ideal companion to whatever you're about to cook and eat. That could be a comforting midweek supper, a special dinner for your favourite people or just a night on the sofa with a box set and snacks.

It doesn't assume you know much about wine, have a big budget or hang out in trendy wine stores. It just assumes you're a greedy person who wants to know more about which wine to drink when but doesn't know where to start.

★ ★ ★

Matching wine with food is often seen as an elite level of wine expertise – something only for the real pros – so why would anyone who doesn't know much about wine go there?

First, there's the additional joy and pleasure you can bring into your life with just a few small changes to something you're already doing. We drink and eat together all the time, but well-matched wine and food are so much more than the sum of their parts. When you pair food and wine thoughtfully, you elevate two already brilliant things to next-level deliciousness – without necessarily spending much more or going to much additional effort.

It's also a chance to eliminate a lot of low-level stress. We've lost count of the messages we've had from friends (hello, everyone) wondering what to serve their in-laws with lunch or what to pick up for a night in with a takeaway and a new boyfriend. If nothing else, hopefully by collecting the most common answers in one book, they'll leave us in peace.

But beyond these immediately practical, short-term fixes, there's also the fact that approaching wine through the food you love to eat is a great way into a world that can often feel vast, impenetrable and riddled with snobbism.

Plenty of people wish they knew more about wine, but it can be daunting. But thinking about what you're going to have for dinner? That's something we all do regularly, and with pleasure. So taking familiar food that you love to cook and eat at home as a starting point will let you get to grips with wine – almost without realising you're doing it. Because the good news is that if you know what you love to eat – and who doesn't? – you're a lot more than halfway to learning what you love to drink. After all, it's still the same process of tasting and enjoying.

Even more helpfully, you'll start to see that many of the reasons that a certain wine goes brilliantly with a certain food are based on principles you probably already understand instinctively when it comes to food: the fact that fish tastes great with lemon, or that there's nothing more moreish than a combination of salty and sweet...

Basically, if you want to get more knowledgeable and comfortable around wine, food can be your gateway drug.

What this book definitely isn't suggesting is that there's any such thing as a 'perfect pairing'. Wine and food are quite literally a matter of taste, which means that everyone's palate is different – there are endless numbers of brilliant combinations out there, and half the fun comes from experimenting and learning what you like. This book is just a collection of the pairings that have brought us the most joy, so they can become delicious shortcuts for you.

None of this is to say that you're doing anything wrong if you pick up a quick bottle of a reliable favourite without thinking, or drink whatever you can find in the house because you haven't been to the shops. Sometimes you have the time and the headspace to think about what you're drinking with your food, and sometimes you don't. And that is totally fine.

But when you are in the mood to choose a wine that will make a meal something to really savour, this book will be your guide.

# How to Use this Book

You can use this purely as a reference book: look up what you're eating, note the wines that go with it best, and head to the shops. Or you can dip in and out at leisure, without any particular food in mind. As you read, you'll absorb lots of useful information about the world of wine, almost without realising it, and in a way that you can easily remember and apply next time you're picking up a bottle.

Upfront is a quick guide to some of the basic terminology that it really is worth having at your fingertips as you find your way around wine, plus a bit of jargon-busting. The pairings are grouped into six sections, arranged by different food and meal types. All the foods are also indexed at the back for speedy reference, too.

At the end of each of these sections are at-a-glance guides covering the main ways to serve some of the most popular meals out there – different takes on pasta, pizza and roast dinners, to name a few.

For other dishes, there are specific, more detailed pairings, which tell you more about one particular wine that works well, and why – as well as giving more general suggestions, under the heading, '**If you can't find this, go for...**'

If you want a really broad, top-line way to describe what you need, perhaps by asking a member of staff in the shop or glancing over a few labels, you'll find that under the heading '**If all else fails, ask for...**'

## But What About Eating Out?

This book is for when you're drinking at home, but what about ordering wine in restaurants? That's a very different situation, which is why we've kept the focus here to times when you have the chance to go shopping for wine yourself.

For one thing, unless you're at a restaurant with a ten-tonne, 300-page list, you'll have far fewer wines to choose from in a restaurant than in a decent-sized shop. More importantly, though, you'll have people there who can help and advise you.

All the same, because we hope this book will give you a thirst for making more informed and interesting choices in restaurants too, turn to pp.167–170 for tips on how to make the most of a restaurant wine list.

# 1

# wine
# basics

# WHAT WINE WORDS MEAN

Most of us aren't used to talking in detail about how things taste or smell: we're far more at ease with describing how things look, for instance. That's one of the reasons why when people talk and write about wine it can feel like they're speaking a totally different language. (To be fair, quite a lot of the words used do actually derive from other languages.)

That's *one* of the reasons, but another is the fact that there are too many people in the world of wine who like to show off and demonstrate their superiority by using words that mark them out as someone who knows their stuff but which 'normal' people wouldn't understand.

So here are some of the most common wine words, as well as what they mean and how they're used, so you can know your stuff, too. Some are genuinely useful and will help you get your hands on the wine you want. Some will just help you see through the bullshit.

## The Basics

### WINE
A drink made from fermented grape juice, with an ABV of 5.5–15.5%. Anything else isn't a wine. That stuff your great-aunt Maud makes out of elderflowers? Not wine.

### WHITE WINE
White wine can be made from white or red grapes. Oh yes. If you press red grapes, you can still end up with white grape juice, because most of the colour is contained in the skins.

## RED WINE

Red wine, you may be relieved to learn, has to be made from red grapes. The colour – and some other interesting and tasty things like tannins (see p.23) – comes from the skins of the grapes, which are left in contact with the juice after the fruit is pressed.

## ROSÉ/PINK WINE

Pink wine is white wine that's halfway to becoming red wine (not a mix of white and red wines). If leaving red grape skins in contact with the juice for long enough makes a red wine, leaving them there for less time makes a pink wine. The longer the skins are left with the juice, the deeper the colour – just like making a cup of tea and leaving the tea bag in longer for a darker, stronger flavour.

## ORANGE WINE

Orange wine is a kind of white wine, made with white grapes but treated as if they were being used to make a red wine. That means the skins are left in contact with the juice during the winemaking process to give a pinkish-orange colour to the final result, and more body and tannins to the wine. It can also be referred to as 'skin-contact wine'. This is an ancient method of making wine that was revived in the 1990s by trendy experimental winemakers. Orange wine is not made from oranges.

## FORTIFIED WINE

Fortified wines are wines that have had a spirit (such as brandy) added to them during the winemaking process: famous examples include port and sherry.

The addition of a spirit has two consequences. The first, pretty obvious, consequence is that the wine ends up stronger, thanks to the extra booze: fortified wines usually clock in around 20% ABV. The second, less obvious consequence is that the wine ends up sweeter. Why? It's all to do with when the spirit is added. As wine ferments, the natural sugars in it are converted to alcohol by yeasts, turning it from grape juice into wine. When you add a spirit before the fermentation process is complete, you kill the yeast and stop the fermentation, meaning that sugar that would otherwise have been turned into alcohol remains in the wine to sweeten it.

All that extra alcohol and sugar means that fortified wines keep for longer than other wines, and that's precisely why the process was invented, hundreds of years ago: as a method of preserving wine that had to travel a long way by sea before being drunk.

# Talking About Where Wine Comes From

### PROTECTED DESIGNATION OF ORIGIN (PDO)

A Protected Designation of Origin is a mark of origin that can be applied to a whole range of European produce, including wine. A PDO guarantees that a product has been made in a particular locality or region, according to the traditions of that region, and is carefully regulated by European Union law. Basically, then, PDOs work as a kind of 'accept no substitutions' system.

In different languages, the phrase PDO appears in different guises: it becomes DOC/DOCG in Italy, DO/DOCA in Spain, and AOP in France (where it's replaced an older system called AOC, in case you see that anywhere). You might also hear the French word 'appellation' used to mean much the same thing: this just means 'name' (*je m'appelle* and all that) and is taken from the French version of the phrase. The American equivalent is an AVA.

When it comes to wine, a PDO covers the kinds of grapes that are used to make wine, plus the winemaking style, all of which will shape the end result. This means that wines with the same PDO will have a lot in common, as they're made with the same grapes, and in the same style. If you know the PDO – for example, Beaujolais, in France – you can tell broadly what the wine will be like, because for a wine to receive the

Beaujolais PDO (or AOP, in French), it must be made from the Gamay grape, which makes light-bodied red wines that are best drunk young. Of course, there are many other factors at play that create variations between wines from a single PDO, from the year the grapes were harvested, to the different micro-climates and geographies within the region, to the tastes and preferences of the winemaker, even when working in a defined local tradition.

Many wine producers, especially from traditional wine-producing countries, will only label their wines based on where they're from, using this as a shorthand for the grapes and the winemaking style. One obvious problem with this is that it requires you to remember the different winemaking rules of each area in order to get a sense of what a wine will be like – and that's a big ask.

Wines from countries that are newer to the winemaking game (for example, Australia, South Africa and the USA) are usually labelled straightforwardly with the grape varieties as well as their place of origin. This makes it much less daunting to buy wines from these countries, which puts their producers at an advantage when selling to a wider audience.

That's spurred some winemakers and marketing boards working within traditional regional labelling systems to face up to how unhelpful their approach can be. More and more of them are labelling their bottles with additional useful details, so you don't need to memorise the local traditions to understand what you're buying.

A second problem with the PDO system – this time for winemakers – is that what's meant as a way to preserve local traditions and provide a certain guarantee of quality can also act as a straitjacket for anyone who wants to experiment with new ways of doing things. These rebel winemakers often work outside the system, giving us the chance to drink creative and innovative wines alongside the traditions protected and preserved by the PDO classification.

## DOMAINE

The estate or property on which the wine was made – not necessarily where the grapes were grown, as estates will often gather fruit from lots of different places to make their wine.

## BLEND OR CEPAGE

The combination of different grapes used to make a wine. Most wines are a blend of different kinds of grape, to add complexity and combine flavours that complement each other.

## VINTAGE/NON-VINTAGE/MULTI-VINTAGE

A 'vintage' is a year, and some years are better for making wine than others. A 'vintage wine' is made from grapes harvested in the same year. 'Non-vintage' (or NV) wines are made by blending wines from different years: confusingly, this doesn't necessarily mean that these wines are younger than a vintage wine, just that they're not made from a single vintage.

## NATURAL

Natural wine has become achingly trendy in recent years, with specialist natural wine lists, wine bars and wine festivals cropping up across the world – but what is it?

The first thing to clarify is that natural wine isn't a particular style of wine – that is, it doesn't describe the way a wine tastes. Natural wine can be red, white, rosé or orange, still or sparkling. You can no more know how a wine will taste based on the fact that it's described as natural than you can know how any other wine will taste based purely on the fact that it's a 'regular' wine.

Instead, natural winemaking describes an ambition for how wine is made: from the way the grapes are farmed and harvested, to the fermentation and bottling. The movement developed over the last few decades as a reaction against modern, industrialised, mass-produced methods of wine production that natural winemakers argue are detrimental both to the environment and to the quality of the wines we drink. But, unlike labels such as 'organic' or 'biodynamic', there's no regulation defining what a natural wine is, or what can and can't officially be labelled as natural, so everything is a question of interpretation and sliding scales.

The word 'ambition' is important here. Natural winemakers aim to make their wines with as little intervention as possible. This may include working with minimal chemical pesticides, using traditional farming methods, working relatively small parcels of land so that they don't have to use industrial harvesting machinery, or allowing the fermentation process to run its course without using the stabilising and preserving processes that have been introduced to winemaking over the decades to guarantee reliable consistency. (Some of the world's oldest and most traditional estates have a lot in common with natural winemakers, simply because they never modernised their methods!)

Natural winemakers may also be committed to certifiably organic or bio-dynamic methods, or both: biodynamic farming is a particular approach to sustainability that goes further than organic farming and which has its own set of rules and methods. However, not all organic or biodynamic wines are natural wines: they're not the same thing.

Every natural winemaker will interpret the idea slightly differently, and be at a different point in their winemaking journey. A process that one natural winemaker accepts might be decried by another. And a winemaker may well be aiming to significantly reduce the amount of interventions they make in the process, but not yet have got as far as they want. That's why natural winemaking is best described as an ambition – something winemakers are exploring and working towards – rather than any locked-down definition.

Because of this ambiguity, there are a few common myths about natural wine that deserve to be busted.

The first is that all natural wines taste 'funky' – maybe more like cider. Some do, but some taste very much like you'd expect any other wine to taste.

Funkiness is not a defining quality of natural wine. If you like that style of wine, simply ask for it, rather than asking for a natural wine.

The second big myth is that natural wines don't give you hangovers. This is a brilliantly wishful bit of thinking based on the fact that most natural winemakers add lower levels of sulphites than you'll find in 'regular' wines. (Sulphites are common food preservatives – found in dried apricots, for instance – that are added to wine to prevent it from oxidising, to keep the appearance and taste fresh.) People believe that sulphites give you a hangover, so, according to that thinking, a low or no sulphite wine = no hangover.

Sadly, it's alcohol that causes hangovers, not sulphites, as you'll discover if you spend a night downing gin or vodka, which are usually sulphite-free, but certainly not hangover-free. (A very small percentage of the population are sensitive to sulphites, which is why their presence is marked on packaging, but that's a different story.) If you want to reduce your chances of a sore head the next day, the surest approach is to reduce your alcohol consumption by seeking out wines with a low ABV – say, 5.5–12% rather than 13–16% – or, of course, just by drinking less.

Fundamentally, the best reason to seek out natural wines is if you share the movement's anti-industrialising philosophy of farming and food production. Whatever matters most to you about the wine you drink and the story behind it, there are many great, well-made wines that aren't natural wines, and not every natural wine is great – so the best way to drink well is to stay curious, and be open-minded.

## TERROIR

A strong contender for the most pretentious wine word of them all. It's a French word that's almost impossible to translate because it's a very French idea. 'Terroir' literally means 'soil' or 'land', so you can think of it as describing the patch of land on which the wine grapes were grown. But terroir really means more than that. It reflects the belief that produce (and the things made from that produce, like wine) capture and reflect the particular characteristics of that precise area of land – the nature of the soil, its climate and geography, the things that grow there, and even the character of the people who live there. It's as if the land has an essence, spirit or personality that it lends to everything that comes from there. That personality is terroir.

### VARIETY
A kind of grape. These, naturally, tend to have different names in different countries. Pinot Gris, for instance, is one popular French grape variety that's called Pinot Grigio in Italy.

## Talking About Flavour

### ACIDITY
Quite simply, how acidic a wine is. Acidity makes your mouth water – literally – and is what makes foods like lemons taste sour. A little acidity in a wine makes the overall flavour well balanced. NB: acidity is not the opposite of sweetness; some wines are both sweet and acidic – like Sauternes, a famous sweet wine from France. (Think of pancakes with lemon juice and sugar. The lemon isn't the exact opposite of the sweetness – it doesn't cancel it out, but balances and complements it, so you get the experience of both sweet and sharp together.)

### SWEET/DRY
In wine, these words are opposites. (Yes, wet is usually the opposite of dry, and savoury is usually the opposite of sweet. But that would be too easy, wouldn't it?) They're both ways of talking about how much sugar there is in a wine.

Grapes are very sugary, and most of that sugar gets converted into alcohol in the winemaking process – but not all of it. That's why you'll hear people talk about 'residual sugar' – it's what's left over after the rest has been turned into alcohol. A sweet wine has high levels of residual sugar; a dry wine has low levels. Then there are wines that fall in between – medium-dry, etc.

'Dry' is one of the most misunderstood terms in wine: the majority of wines sold are dry wines, in line with current tastes. Basically, unless you're drinking a dessert wine, you're likely to be drinking a dry or at most off-dry wine. (Something to bear in mind next time someone asks if you're doing dry January...)

### TANNIC/TANNINS

Tannins are chemical compounds found in grape skins, stalks and seeds. They create a slightly drying, bitter, puckering sensation in your mouth, which, in the right amounts, make a wine more interesting. While all wines contain some tannins, it's really only something that matters and that you'll notice in red wines.

If this all sounds a bit mysterious, think of tea – another familiar plant with tannins in it. The longer you leave tea to brew, the more bitter it will taste ... and it's exactly the same with grapes and wine.

### FRUITY

All wine is made from grape juice, and grapes are fruit, so surely all wine tastes fruity? Well, arguably – but some wines taste more fruity than others. This is a way to talk about flavours that might remind you of berries, plums, peaches, pears, apples, pineapples ... or a whole range of other fruit.

### EARTHY

A way to describe certain types of flavours. Some wines taste slightly mushroomy or can remind you of the smell of wet leaves, or soil – these flavours are said to be 'earthy'.

### MINERAL/MINERALITY

Like 'fruity' or 'earthy', this is a metaphor for describing a family of flavours that occur in some wines. When the taste of a wine reminds you of the way that chalk, stone, pebbles or flint smell (assuming you've never put any of those in your mouth), you could describe it as having minerality.

## VEGETAL
Does a wine remind you of the flavour of vegetables in some way? Then it's 'vegetal'.

## OAK/OAKY/OAKED
Some wines (red and white) are stored in oak barrels (oaked) as part of the winemaking process, which means they absorb some of the flavour and aroma of the wood. The newer the barrel, the more of its flavour it gives to the wine. Winemakers can cheat by literally adding chips of oak to vats of wine, but this is a cheap trick that mostly makes for unpleasant and unbalanced wines. Done carefully, oaking contributes to some of the world's greatest wines – for example, Barolo or Grand Cru Burgundy. Signs that a wine has been in contact with oak include notes of vanilla, coconut, smokiness, toffee and even chocolate.

## TART
A tart wine is an ever so slightly sour wine – think of biting into a plum that isn't ripe yet. That might sound horrible, but sometimes it can really work, and remind you of other (delicious) tart flavours like grapefruit. But it can also be unpleasant, and a sign that the grapes were harvested before they were ripe.

## SAVOURY
Savoury wines have vegetal or earthy flavours and aromas, as opposed to fruitier notes.

## CRISP, SMOOTH…?
Blah blah blah. These words have no real agreed meaning. They're mostly just padding on the back of the bottle or a menu because someone couldn't think of anything more interesting or useful to say.

# Talking About What a Wine is Like to Drink

## ABV

'Alcohol by volume' – displayed as a percentage on every bottle of wine. Any wine at or above 15% ABV is considered pretty punchy in terms of alcohol content.

## FINISH

Not something to put in your dishwasher: the finish is the flavours that are left lingering in your mouth after you've swallowed the wine. Good wines tend to have a 'long finish' – that is, you experience a range of flavours well after you've swallowed a mouthful.

## STRUCTURE

The way the different elements in a wine work together and the way they unfold – just as we'd talk about the structure of an argument, story or play. Do you get one flavour first, then another? The very best wines have complex structures. A simple wine doesn't have much structure, it just does one thing. That doesn't mean that simple wines can't be enjoyable to drink: sometimes simple is exactly what you want.

## BALANCE

A well-balanced wine has all its different flavours and characteristics working well together – like singers in perfect harmony. The different elements that should balance out are acidity, sweetness, tannins, fruit and savoury flavours. (Those words are all explained here.)

## BODY

Think of this like weight categories in boxing: 'body' is wine talk for how light or powerful the flavour and impact of a wine are. Light-bodied wines produce a less powerful sensation in your mouth (a good example is the French wine, Beaujolais), while heavy-bodied wines pack a serious punch in your mouth – for instance, an Italian Amarone. You can probably guess what medium-bodied wines are like. A good comparison is to think of the difference between skimmed milk and cream – one is very light in your mouth while one is much heavier. A whole range of factors can influence how full-bodied a wine is, from the grapes used to the climate in which they're grown.

### NOSE

How a wine smells. Some wines have a really strong smell/nose/aroma that you can pick up with a single sniff over a glass, and some have barely any aroma at all, even though they pack a good flavour punch. Why? Just as some flowers smell more strongly than others, some grapes are simply more aromatic than others.

### LEGS

This is proper old-boys-club stuff. When you swirl a wine in the glass and let it run down the side, some wines will stick to the glass more, leaving distinct streaks, because they're slightly thicker. Those streaks are the 'legs', and are usually a sign that the wine is higher in alcohol – which means it's likely to be punchier to drink. Before modern labelling, this was a useful way to estimate a wine's ABV. These days, now that wines all have their alcohol content listed on the bottle, you can just check the label...

### MOUTHFEEL

A weird word that means just what it says – the way that a wine feels in your mouth. Think of the contrast between a thick gravy or a thin sauce – the way they coat your mouth differently. That's mouthfeel.

## Talking About Quality

### MATURE

Wine takes time: a mature wine is one that has been left long enough to be good to drink – it's the wine equivalent of being ripe. This is a pretty subjective way to think about wine and the kind of thing that experts will fight over.

## COMPLEX

A wine that has a lot of flavours in it – a lot going on. The best-quality wines tend to be the most complex.

## FAULTY

When a wine isn't as it ought to be. If you don't know a particular wine well it can be hard to judge this, but if you've drunk something before and it tastes different this time – and not for the better – then it's probably faulty (and you have every right to take it or send it back).

## FLAT

Not (necessarily) to do with fizz. A 'flat' wine is one that's been left open for too long, so it has lost the best of its flavours.

## THIN

A wine that tastes watery, without much flavour, can be described as 'thin'.

## CLOSED/OPEN

In wine speak, this doesn't mean literally whether the bottle is closed or open (although here's a pro tip: opening the bottle is a great way to get more out of your wine). A 'closed' wine is one where the flavours aren't as well developed as they should be. That might be because it needs to be left longer in the bottle – for months or even years longer in some cases – or because it hasn't been left to breathe (see the entry on 'breathing'). An open wine, on the other hand, has all its flavours coming through nicely.

## CORKED/CORK TAINT/TCA

If a bottle has a faulty cork it will make the wine taste, quite frankly, gross – sort of cardboardy. Of course, if you don't know how a wine is meant to taste, it's hard to say for sure if it's corked, but never be afraid to get a waiter or sommelier to check and give you their opinion. If you think it tastes horrible, it probably isn't right.

# Serving Wine

### DECANT/DECANTER
Decanting a wine means pouring the bottle into another container before you pour it into a glass. A decanter is a special kind of wine jug designed for that purpose – although you can use any regular water jug, to be honest. Any kind of wine – red, white, rosé, or even sparkling – might benefit from decanting depending on circumstances.

You decant wine for several reasons. One, because it has tiny bits in it (called sediment) which you can leave behind in the bottle. This more commonly applies to red wines. Two, because it needs to 'breathe' – see below. Three, because it's a bit too chilled and you need to warm it up quickly: pouring the liquid into a new, room-temperature container will help take the chill off it more quickly than leaving it in the cold bottle.

### BREATHING
Some wines need to breathe to be at their best – that is, they need to come into contact with the air so they can react with the oxygen. This helps their flavours 'develop', or come through more when you drink them. You can help this process simply by swirling the wine in your glass (try not to get it everywhere). Some wines benefit more from being left to breathe than others: if you're at a restaurant, the sommelier will probably let you know.

### SOMMELIER
This word originally meant 'butler' – the person in a large household who was responsible for choosing, storing and serving wine. And that's still what a sommelier does today, only in a restaurant. A sommelier is there to serve you – to help you make the right choice, whatever your budget or level of knowledge. Snooty, old-school sommeliers who make you feel inferior are dinosaurs who should hurry up and become extinct. For tips on how to get the most out of chatting to a sommelier, see pp.167–170.

2

# home-cooked classics

Comfort food, familiar favourites, family recipes – these are the meals we've all got in our weekly repertoires and that we return to time and time again. They're dependable, unfussy dishes that don't let you down – meals you've made so often you probably don't need a written recipe to whip them up.

There's a good argument that says that the everyday, ordinary things in our lives are exactly the things that deserve the most care and attention. What we do, touch and come into contact with most frequently is what has the biggest impact on the quality of our life. Food and wine are no different.

What's good is too good to be saved for a rare and distant 'best' or special occasion – and that goes for a thoughtfully chosen, well-matched bottle of wine with your food. The meals you eat most often at home are just as deserving of the right bottle of wine as those you eat occasionally on high days and holidays, for the exact reason that you eat them more often.

So it's well worth getting to know the wines that take your familiar favourites to the next level. Depending on what you eat most often at home, some of these wines have the potential to become your own 'house wines'. Once you've tried a bottle, you might even want to order a case of those that are best matched with the recipes you cook most often. Always having the right wine on hand will keep life simple and introduce that comforting, familiar element that most of us want from home-cooked classics – plus it'll make the particular pleasure of good wine matched with good food part of the fabric of everyday life, which is just as it should be.

# Sausage, Mash & Gravy + South African Shiraz

WHAT'S THE WINE?

A red wine made in South Africa from the Shiraz grape (which is also known as Syrah). This grape was first planted in South Africa in the 1890s, and the country now makes wines of incredible quality and elegance. Some of the best regions – and therefore the names to look out for on a label – are Swartland and Stellenbosch.

WHY THIS WINE?

Sausage and mash is nothing without its gravy, and that's a game-changer when it comes to finding the perfect wine match: a good gravy is rich and intensely savoury, so it needs a powerful wine to take it on. A South African Shiraz brings its own warm, smoky flavours into play, as well as the distinctive delicate, spicy, cracked black pepper notes that this grape is known for – just like a sprinkling of fresh black pepper over your plate, it'll perk up and enhance this comfort food no end. If you're someone who believes that sausage and mash isn't complete without ketchup, you'll be pleased to know that the rich red fruit flavours of the Shiraz will act like a sweet-but-tart dollop of tomato sauce.

IF YOU CAN'T FIND THIS, GO FOR…

A Syrah/Shiraz from France's Rhône Valley or one from Australia.

IF ALL ELSE FAILS, ASK FOR…

A spicy, medium-bodied red.

# Chilli + Napa Valley Zinfandel

A red wine from Napa in California, made with the Zinfandel grape. Zinfandel is originally from Croatia, where it's called Tribidrag or Crljenak Kaštelanski – names that are almost as much of a mouthful as the wine. You'll also find it grown in southern Italy, where it's called Primitivo ... just to keep you on your toes.

There's a secret tip for making good chilli that pretty much everyone must know by now, even if they haven't tried it: grating a few squares of super-dark chocolate into your chilli just before serving to give it an even richer flavour. This really does work and one of the reasons it does is because sweetness complements and enhances spicy foods. The exact same thinking lies behind this food-and-wine combo, which works for both veggie and beef versions of the dish.

The grape known as Zinfandel in California ('Zin' to its friends) was first planted there in 1829 and now makes some of the finest, most complex and powerful red wines in the world: true American classics that are spicy, layered and intense, just like your chilli. But Zinfandel's brilliance doesn't stop there. In addition to all those full-on flavours, it has a fruity sweetness – almost like baked plums or blackberry crumble. This works in just the same way as that dark chocolate – enhancing the heat of the dish, and letting the combination of slow-cooked spices sing.

A Zinfandel from the Sierra Foothills or Lodi regions, both also in California; a Primitivo from Puglia, in Italy; or a South African Syrah/Shiraz from the Stellenbosch region.

A spicy, full-bodied red wine with lots of fruit character.

# Meatloaf + Mendocino County Cabernet Franc

**WHAT'S THE WINE?**
A red wine from Mendocino County in California, made with the Cabernet Franc grape.

The Cabernet Franc-based wines being produced in California today by a new generation of winemakers are increasingly in a style all their own, rather than trying to ape the traditional European styles: new American classics, to drink with a classic American meal.

**WHY THIS WINE?**
Every meatloaf fan (no, not that Meatloaf) knows that this old-school American comfort food isn't complete without a good splodge of ketchup on the plate.

It might sound strange, but the same principles are at play when you drink a Cabernet Franc – you're adding a soft, slightly spicy fruitiness to complement the well-seasoned, savoury meatloaf. You might even get a little whiff of that earthy tomato-skin smell from your glass, too – the ideal combo with meatloaf.

**IF YOU CAN'T FIND THIS, GO FOR…**
A wine made in France's Loire Valley from the Cabernet Franc grape or a Syrah/Shiraz-based wine from Stellenbosch in South Africa.

**IF ALL ELSE FAILS, ASK FOR…**
A spicy and earthy medium-bodied red wine.

# Corned Beef Hash + Valpolicella Classico

## WHAT'S THE WINE?

An Italian red from the Veneto region in the north-east of the country, made from a blend of various local grapes. (The name Valpolicella means 'the valley of many cellars', because so many wines are made there.) The 'Classico' bit of the name tells you that the wine has been made in the traditional way, which keeps it extremely light – some of these wines are almost like a dark rosé in colour. They're best served slightly chilled, so pop the bottle in the fridge for 30–45 minutes before you want to drink it.

## WHY THIS WINE?

This is a very salty, savoury dish – the 'corned' in the name refers to the large grains of salt used to preserve the meat. Normally with salted and preserved meats a white wine is a good bet. But the big, beefy flavour of this dish, not to mention all the other garnishes and toppings that go into a hash – onions, Worcestershire sauce, mustard or whatever else you like to add – means it calls for a red.

As with so many pairings, it's helpful to think about what dressing or garnish would go with the food, then use wine in the same way. Corned beef hash is brilliant with lots of ketchup, so a wine with acidity and tart red fruit flavours is the one – and that's what you get from a Valpolicella Classico.

## IF YOU CAN'T FIND THIS, GO FOR...

A red from the Beaujolais region of France, a wine made in Burgundy from Pinot Noir, or a Cinsault – again from France.

## IF ALL ELSE FAILS, ASK FOR...

A lighter-bodied red wine with lots of crunchy, red fruit flavours.

# Moussaka + Assyrtiko

### WHAT'S THE WINE?
A white wine from Santorini, made from the Assyrtiko grape.

### WHY THIS WINE?
A Greek meal is a great excuse to try a Greek wine – it's a crying shame that they're not better known or more widely drunk, as wines have been made in this part of the world for thousands of years.

Moussaka is a particularly rich and comforting dish, with the unusual warmth of cinnamon giving even greater sweetness to the lamb (or beef, or veal, depending on who you ask) and the slow-cooked, wine-laced tomato sauce. You can use the remainder of an open bottle of basic red in the sauce, if you have any lying around (there's no point cooking with anything too good), but you'll want something fresh and white in your glass to balance out the full flavours of the food.

Grown on the steep slopes of the volcanic island under the brilliant, purifying Greek sun, the vines on Santorini are kept cool by the strong winds that blow over the Aegean Sea and right across the island. The result is wines that are beautifully fresh – a Mediterranean breeze in a glass to brighten up dinner.

### IF YOU CAN'T FIND THIS, GO FOR...
A dry German Riesling or a Riesling from Australia's Clare Valley.

### IF ALL ELSE FAILS, ASK FOR...
A clean, dry white wine with acidity and power.

# Lasagne + Aglianico

### WHAT'S THE WINE?
A red wine from the southern Italian region of Campania, made from the Aglianico grape. This is a hot, dry part of the world, and all that sun makes for a rich, powerful wine.

### WHY THIS WINE?
Lasagne delivers on big flavours, thanks to the tomatoes, beef and cheese, but in particular, thanks to the slow cooking they all get once layered between the pasta sheets, which intensifies them and brings the dish together. This all calls for a good, punchy red. Italy isn't short on those, but since Naples – regional capital of Campania – is one of the places that claims to have invented lasagne, it feels only natural to wash it down with one of the area's wines.

Aglianico wines are full of complexity, just like a decent lasagne, while good levels of acidity will cut through the richness of the food and refresh your palate between bites.

### IF YOU CAN'T FIND THIS, GO FOR...
Other Italian reds will go down a treat, too: try one made from the Primitivo grape, wines from the Etna region, or a Montepulciano from the Abruzzo region.

### IF ALL ELSE FAILS, ASK FOR...
A rich, bold, Italian red from the south of the country.

# Pasta Bolognese + Montepulciano d'Abruzzo

A red from the Abruzzo region of Italy, made mostly from the Montepulciano grape but blended with a few other varieties. (Watch out that you don't mistake Montepulciano for the very similar-sounding Montalcino – a town in Tuscany that also produces excellent wines.)

A good ragù Bolognese is simple, but not quick, to make, so when it comes to this pairing, we're not talking about a pack of mince and a jar of sauce stirred together for a few minutes. The long, slow, real thing is an intensely savoury combination of meat (beef, veal, pork – recipes vary) cooked until it melts down, plus a relatively light touch with the tomatoes.

Italian reds are almost universally brilliant with food – they're more or less designed to be drunk as part of a meal – because of their good levels of acidity. This wine is no different, while its full body and good levels of tannins will be a proper match for the full-on flavours of a real ragù Bolognese.

When it comes to the flavours you'll find in your glass, some food and wine combinations are all about contrast, but in this case the dish and drink have lots in common. Montepulciano wines have their own hint of tomato but also a fragrant, fresh, herby note – something like oregano or basil. To all that you're also adding lots of red fruit flavours that will intensify and complement the tomato in your ragù.

An Italian Barbera or a wine from France's Côtes du Rhône region.

A medium-bodied Italian red with herbal notes.

# Spaghetti & Meatballs + Chianti

## WHAT'S THE WINE?
An Italian red from the Chianti region, in Tuscany, usually made with a blend of red grapes.

## WHY THIS WINE?
It's easy to overlook how acidic tomato sauce is. We don't think of it that way, but canned tomatoes in particular – the basis for most tomato pasta sauces – have both a good dose of natural sugar and significant levels of acidity. This means you need a wine with good acidity to match, so it won't be completely overwhelmed by the sauce.

You'll also want a wine to match the character of the food. This is unpretentious, hearty family fare for when you want cheering up and feeding up, so the wine can't be pretentious or flimsy.

The red wines of the Chianti region are the ones you used to see served with those faintly ridiculous straw covers in old-school trattorias – exactly the sort of place you can imagine folk tucking into spaghetti and meatballs. What's more, they have great acidity for that sauce, enough body to stand up to the savoury flavours of the meatballs and Parmesan, and lots of red fruit and ripe tomato flavours of their own.

## IF YOU CAN'T FIND THIS, GO FOR...
Any Italian wine made from the Sangiovese grape, a Rosso di Montalcino from Tuscany, or almost any Italian red made from a blend of Syrah and Merlot grapes.

## IF ALL ELSE FAILS, ASK FOR...
A medium-bodied Italian red with tart fruit flavours and pleasant acidity.

# Seafood Pasta + Fiano

### WHAT'S THE WINE?

A white wine made from the Fiano grape in the ridiculously beautiful coastal Italian region of Campania, whose capital is Naples. This was the grape of choice for the Ancient Romans, who knew a thing or two about feasting with wine. If you can find it, look out for Fiano di Avellino, which is one of the best examples out there – the volcanic hillsides of Avellino make for particularly interesting and delicious wines.

### WHY THIS WINE?

As is so often the case, food and wine that are born out of similar conditions make great partners – a classic Italian seafood dish and a classic Italian wine made on the cliffs of the Campanian coast. Fiano wines have such bright, zesty lemon flavours that they call to mind the beautiful fragrant Amalfi lemons that also hail from Campania: this makes them the perfect foil for seafood of all kinds.

### IF YOU CAN'T FIND THIS, GO FOR...

A white wine made from Vermentino, Soave or Sauvignon Blanc grapes.

### IF ALL ELSE FAILS, ASK FOR...

A fresh, lemony, zesty, textured white wine.

# Fish Cakes + Ligurian White

WHAT'S THE WINE?
A white wine from the northern Italian coastal region of Liguria. Most are made with a significant percentage of the local Vermentino and Pigato grapes. If you can, look for the name Colli di Luni on the bottle: this part of Liguria makes especially interesting wines with at least 35 percent Vermentino.

WHY THIS WINE?
Bulked out with so much potato, fish cakes have a relatively delicate flavour, which is why they're such great comfort food. It also means they need a wine that won't overpower them.

The region of Liguria has a long tradition of making light, easy to drink white wines, which the locals drink with fried fish – Liguria is as famous for its fritto misto (fried mixed seafood) as it is for its wine. So it's no surprise that wines from this part of the world go brilliantly with breaded, fried fish cakes, too. They're the perfect combination of delicate flavour, light body and a zippy citrus edge that will act like a squeeze of fresh lemon over your fish cakes.

IF YOU CAN'T FIND THIS, GO FOR…
A Soave, Traminer or Fiano – all Italian whites.

IF ALL ELSE FAILS, ASK FOR…
A fresh, clean Italian white full of lemon flavours.

# Goan Fish Curry + Asti Spumante

## WHAT'S THE WINE?

A sweet, keenly priced Italian sparkling wine ('spumante' is just the Italian for sparkling wine), made from Muscat Blanc grapes. This wine is named after the town of Asti, in the Piedmont (Piemonte in Italian, and possibly therefore on the label too) region, where it's produced.

Asti Spumante also has a relatively low alcohol content – worth remembering in and of itself when you want to take things easy. On first sip you could be forgiven for thinking you've accidentally poured yourself a fruity sparkling soft drink.

## WHY THIS WINE?

A good fish curry has a warming heat to it, which means your wine needs to match not only the relatively delicate flavours of the fish but the spice of the sauce. This is a pairing that will do both, meaning it works a treat with a lot of fish- and chicken-based curries. The bubbles keep your mouth fresh between forkfuls, while the sweet fruitiness of the wine will complement the heat perfectly, showing off both food and wine to best advantage.

## IF YOU CAN'T FIND THIS, GO FOR...

A Moscato d'Asti or a sweeter style of Prosecco.

## IF ALL ELSE FAILS, ASK FOR...

A sweet sparkling wine.

# Moules Marinière + Loire Sauvignon Blanc

**WHAT'S THE WINE?**
A white from France's Loire region made from the Sauvignon Blanc grape.

**WHY THIS WINE?**
Garlic and onions are such familiar ingredients that it's easy to under-estimate how punchy and even slightly bitter they can be. When they're this integral to a relatively pared-back dish that also packs a big hit of protein, you need a wine that can really stand up to them. Anything too simple will be completely overpowered.

Sauvignon Blanc is a grape that's now grown all over the world, but it will taste very different depending on where it's from. When you drink a Sauvignon from France, rather than one from warmer, New World climates such as Australia, you get a wine that still packs a punch but that has an elegant and slightly subtle collection of flavours, including a little citrus for welcome freshness against the creamy sweetness of the mussels. Perhaps most importantly of all, for such a relaxed, slightly messy, preferably cutlery-free meal, these wines are very easy to drink.

(Don't worry too much about the wine you actually cook the mussels in, though – when cooking with wine, while you don't want to use anything truly rancid, you don't need to be too fussy about it. Save your pennies for something good to drink.)

**IF YOU CAN'T FIND THIS, GO FOR…**
A white from Muscadet or a young Chablis – both from France – or a Soave from Italy.

**IF ALL ELSE FAILS, ASK FOR…**
A mineral-rich, fresh white wine.

# Thai Green Curry + Off-Dry Pinot Gris

### WHAT'S THE WINE?
A white wine made from the Pinot Gris grape in the Alsace region of France; for this combination, it's important to look for one labelled 'off-dry'.

You probably recognise the name Pinot Grigio – it's a staple white wine grape on restaurant, bar and pub menus everywhere. Pinot Gris is the exact same grape: Pinot Grigio is its Italian name, while it's known as Pinot Gris in French-speaking regions such as Alsace. It isn't only the name that differs; this grape is treated so differently in Alsace to your typical Italian Pinot Grigio that the resulting wines taste worlds apart.

### WHY THIS WINE?
Whether you make it with chicken, a meaty white fish or as a vegetarian or vegan version, Thai Green Curry is a fresh and fragrant dish that should properly pack a good punch of chilli. To handle that heat you need a little touch of sweetness in your wine. Not a lot – this isn't dessert – but certainly something less than a totally dry wine. That's what off-dry means.

Sugar softens the impact of heat in your mouth and brings out the flavours of spicy ingredients. You won't taste the sweetness, because the two things offset each other so well, but you would notice if your wine was completely dry – because it would taste unpleasant with the spicy food.

### IF YOU CAN'T FIND THIS, GO FOR…
A wine made from the Traminer grape in northern Italy; an off-dry rosé from Provence in France, or from Italy.

### IF ALL ELSE FAILS, ASK FOR…
An off-dry white or a fruity rosé.

# Ratatouille + Côtes de Provence Rosé

## WHAT'S THE WINE?

A rosé wine made in the southern French region Côtes de Provence, from a blend of different grapes. Once, this region had a reputation for producing vast quantities of mediocre wine, but in recent years the quality has shot up.

A quick note on colour: somehow the idea has got round that the paler pink a rosé is, the better its quality. But it isn't that simple – colour isn't in and of itself a guide to quality. In fact, for this pairing you don't want the very palest pink, but something a few shades above. That's a sign that it was left in contact with the skins of the grapes for longer, which will give it more texture and body (see p.26) – perfect if you're drinking it with food.

## WHY THIS WINE?

We're so used to thinking of rosé as a sunny afternoon drink on its own that we don't give it enough credit as a food wine. Even with food, though, it's definitely still a summery style, because pink wines go best with salads and other light vegetable dishes made with summer bounty ... just like ratatouille.

This classic dish also originates from Provence and is all about simplicity. The fresh vegetables, summer herbs and really good olives need a relatively simple and refreshing wine to wash them down. You'll also benefit from a wine with a bit of texture – and this is what you'll get from a rosé (especially a darker-hued one) that you wouldn't from most white wines.

Some rosés can be quite sweet, and this, plus the colour, is supposed to make them more marketable to 'feminine' tastes (ugh). But if you've been put off by the more sickly varieties, don't let that blind you to the refreshing properties of a good dry pink wine with your meal.

## IF YOU CAN'T FIND THIS, GO FOR...

Wines from Provence are widely available, but if you can't find one that appeals you'll also find elegant styles produced in Italy. Although this isn't an exact science, avoid the dark pink bottles if you're not sure.

IF ALL ELSE FAILS, ASK FOR...
A dry, well-made, relatively pale style of rosé from France or Italy.

# Chicken Kiev + Chablis

WHAT'S THE WINE?
A French white wine made in Chablis, in the north of Burgundy, using the Chardonnay grape.

If you come across some punchily priced Chablis when you're browsing the shelves, don't be put off: yes, some of the wines from this region are considered among the best in the world and, as a result, can be very expensive, but there are plenty of delicious but accessible bottles from less well-known winemakers out there, too.

### WHY THIS WINE?
Is it naff? Is it so naff that it's cool again? The classic ready-meal/TV dinner dish that is Chicken Kiev is so delicious that, frankly, who cares? But beloved as it is, there's one thing that this buttery, breadcrumbed flavour bomb is lacking, and that's freshness and acidity.

So that becomes the job for your wine. You'll want to drink the zingiest white you can get your hands on, to cut through all those strong flavours.

Wines from Chablis are about as pure and direct as you can be with Chardonnay: mouthwateringly sharp and lemony-fresh, they're the perfect foil for a puddle of herb butter and have enough body to hold their own against obscene amounts of garlic.

### IF YOU CAN'T FIND THIS, GO FOR...
A Muscadet from France; or Spanish wines from the country's north-west with lots of natural acidity, such as Txakoli or Godello.

### IF ALL ELSE FAILS, ASK FOR...
A fresh and zesty Chardonnay with very subtle (or no) use of oak.

# Caesar Salad + White Rioja

## WHAT'S THE WINE?

A white wine from Spain's Rioja region. This part of the world is most famous for its reds, but about 10 percent of the wines made there are white. The main grape used will be Viura, plus a blend of a real range of others. Riojas of all kinds are typically aged in oak barrels, which gives them a lovely, soft, warm flavour.

## WHY THIS WINE?

The thing that makes a Caesar salad is that famous piquant, salty, zesty dressing. It's so pungent that it needs a very fresh dry wine with lots of texture to drink alongside or the wine will be completely overpowered.

White Riojas have a great natural acidity, which makes them a dream to pair with anything that has a slightly oily texture, such as that Caesar dressing. They're also powerfully flavoured, with lots of mineral accents and a lovely lemony finish, which makes them a refreshing and fitting match for the salty anchovies and cheese that define this dish.

## IF YOU CAN'T FIND THIS, GO FOR...

A Viognier from the Rhône Valley or a Savennières from the Loire Valley, both in France.

## IF ALL ELSE FAILS, ASK FOR...

A textured, rich white wine.

# Macaroni Cheese + Mâconnais

## WHAT'S THE WINE?

A white wine from the Mâconnais, in France – which is in the south of the larger Burgundy winegrowing region. It's made, like most of the best whites from Burgundy, using the Chardonnay grape.

## WHY THIS WINE?

Whether your macaroni cheese uses Cheddar, Gruyère, Parmesan or some secret family combination that you swear by, the only rule here is the cheesier, the better. So you'll need a wine that won't be overpowered by that much oozy, cheesy goodness.

Nobody knows cheese like the French, so it's no surprise that this cheesiest of dishes goes down best with a glass of French white. This is not the time for dainty wine, and a Mâconnais will have plenty of body to stand up to the delicious stodge on your plate, but also some zippy acidity – citrus flavours and fresh green apple – to bring some welcome light relief.

## IF YOU CAN'T FIND THIS, GO FOR…

A Pouilly-Fuissé from France, a Yarra Valley Chardonnay from Australia, or an Elgin Chardonnay from South Africa.

## IF ALL ELSE FAILS, ASK FOR…

A ripe, fruit-forward white wine with good balance and texture.

# Cauliflower Cheese + Red Burgundy

## WHAT'S THE WINE?

A red wine from Burgundy, in France, made with the Pinot Noir grape. Wines labelled Bourgogne Rouge (literally, 'red Burgundy') can be made with grapes from all over the region rather than from very specific single locations. This means they're a relatively affordable way to drink wine from what is otherwise one of the world's most expensive regions.

These wines are light-bodied, which means they're at their best slightly cooler than room temperature: put the bottle in the fridge for 30 minutes before serving and it'll taste so much better.

## WHY THIS WINE?

Let's face it, the cauliflower is just a delivery mechanism for the cheese sauce, so it's the cheesiness that's the main thing to take into account when choosing a wine. But for all that, it's important to remember that this is still a vegetable dish, so the wine shouldn't be anything too heavy or full-bodied.

A simple, classic Pinot Noir will have enough acidity to cut through the super-rich and creamy cheese sauce, with some lovely red fruit flavours – cranberries, raspberries and red cherries – that work almost like a chutney would with cheese. Suddenly, with the addition of the right glass of wine, a super-simple meal becomes something very interesting indeed.

## IF YOU CAN'T FIND THIS, GO FOR…

A wine from France's Alsace region made from the Pinot Noir grape, an English Pinot Noir (the still, not the sparkling variety), or a Triomphe Red, again from Alsace.

## IF ALL ELSE FAILS, ASK FOR…

A simple, light-bodied red wine with red fruit flavours.

# Mushroom Risotto + Barolo

## WHAT'S THE WINE?

A red wine from the Italian region of Piedmont that's made exclusively from the Nebbiolo grape.

Barolo is often referred to in Italy as the king of wines, and the most sought-after bottles are among the most expensive wines in the world: their international success has transformed the fortunes of the region. Despite this, you can still find well-priced bottles, but if you're looking for something even more affordable, look out for alternatives such as Langhe Nebbiolo. Made from the same grape, these wines are nicknamed Baby Barolos for a reason: you'll get much the same experience, but at a lower price point.

## WHY THIS WINE?

Nebbiolo-based wines are known in their homeland for going well with really earthy flavours – notably white truffles, another speciality of the Piedmont region. Since such delicacies are well out of the reach of most of us, you might wonder why that matters. Well, it's because mushrooms have their own beautiful earthiness, meaning Nebbiolo does a great job with them as well.

If your risotto is laced with plenty of Parmesan, the savoury richness of the cheese will be balanced perfectly by the powerful tannins and the uniquely intense fruit found in these very special wines. You'll be left with the elegant and unusually pure fruit notes that are particular to Nebbiolo – raspberry, plum, rose and a hint of liquorice.

## IF YOU CAN'T FIND THIS, GO FOR...

Alternative Italian reds include Barbaresco or Langhe Nebbiolo, as mentioned above. Or try wines from Australia and Mexico made from Nebbiolo.

## IF ALL ELSE FAILS, ASK FOR...

An earthy, medium-bodied red with good tannin structure.

# PIES at a glance

Pork

Fish

Steak
& Ale

Mushroom

Chicken

Shepherd's

Game

# TRY

| | |
|---|---|
| Sherry | Fino<br>Manzanilla |
| Zesty & Fresh White | Chablis<br>Sauvignon Blanc<br>Riesling |
| Textured White | White Rioja<br>Viognier<br>Chardonnay |
| Cheese & Onion | |
| Light-Bodied Red | Pinot Noir<br>Dolcetto<br>Valpolicella |
| Medium-Bodied Red | Merlot<br>Malbec<br>Sangiovese |

# PASTA at a glance

Pesto

Mediterranean Vegetables

Carbonara

Just Parmesan

Tomato & Basil

Ragù

Spicy Tomato

# TRY

| | | |
|---|---|---|
| Easy-Drinking White | | Pinot Grigio<br>Muscadet<br>Vermentino |
| Medium White | | Albariño<br>Sauvignon Blanc<br>Soave |
| Complex White | | Chardonnay<br>Viognier<br>Semillon |
| Rosé | | Provence<br>California<br>Italy |
| Light-Bodied Red | | Pinot Noir<br>Dolcetto<br>Beaujolais |
| Medium-Bodied Red | | Merlot<br>Malbec<br>Grenache |
| Full-Bodied Red | | Cabernet Sauvignon<br>Shiraz<br>Tempranillo |

3

# takeaways
# and
# fast food

When you're in the mood for a takeaway or grabbing something to go, you don't have to put any effort into preparing the food, so you can put that saved time and energy towards choosing a bottle of wine instead.

Sure, that won't be all the time, but there's something fun in the contrast when you eat a hot dog or a hamburger with a good bottle of wine that you've picked out specially.

It's also a chance to prove that wine doesn't only belong with refined and elegant foods. It's a drink that can enhance even the simplest and least pretentious food, and the most relaxed meals. These are indulgent foods that we turn to when we want a particular kind of super-relaxed treat, and what could be more indulgent and relaxing than adding a bottle of wine?

That said, not all takeaway food is a guilty pleasure. The massive rise in the reach and ambition of the food delivery market now means that most of us can get restaurant-style food from a huge range of cuisines brought to our homes. Staying in with a quality takeaway is often a smart, money-saving alternative to date night or a family dinner out at a restaurant.

You'd probably get a decent bottle of wine with dinner if you were eating out. If you're staying in, you can do even better – spending less to get a nicer bottle, and in all likelihood choosing from a bigger selection in a shop than on a wine list, so you can pick a wine that will really do your dinner justice.

# Hot Dog + Verdejo

WHAT'S THE WINE?

A white wine from north-west Spain made using the local Verdejo grape. This grape is a real jack of all trades – it can make classy, quality wines or casual everyday bottles.

The vines in this region include some of the oldest in Europe because, unlike vines in France and Italy, they escaped being wiped out by a pest in the nineteenth century. Old vines make beautifully concentrated flavours, and you'll often pay a premium for wines made from old-vine grapes. But because Verdejo isn't particularly well known, you've got a good chance of a) picking up a real bargain, and b) discovering a new favourite grape.

WHY THIS WINE?

Imagine a classic hot dog with fried onions and a squiggle of tangy, sweet yellow mustard. The dominant flavours are really that onion and mustard, over and above the Frankfurter sausage and bun. The spicy mustard needs a wine with high acidity to match (mustard itself is actually pretty acidic), while the green, herby notes of the wine will be a perfect complement for the onions. You'll also get a bright lime flavour coming through, which will keep you refreshed as you dig in. All in all, this is an unfussy, relaxed, easy-drinking wine – what more could you want with a hot dog?

IF YOU CAN'T FIND THIS, GO FOR...

A white wine made with the Albariño, Colombard or Pinot Grigio grapes.

IF ALL ELSE FAILS, ASK FOR...

A fresh, zesty white wine that's refreshing and easy to drink.

# Hamburger + Red Bordeaux

### WHAT'S THE WINE?
A red wine from the Bordeaux region of south-west France. There's no getting away from the fact that Bordeaux is one of the most important, but also one of the stuffiest, most expensive and complicated wine-producing regions in the world. It's easy to imagine that Bordeaux wines are only for rich old people in wood-panelled restaurants, but that really isn't true.

These wines became so desirable because they're so good – and armed with a little knowledge you can find delicious and affordable bottles. Wine at all price points is made in Bordeaux. To avoid paying for a big name, look for wines from the lesser-known areas of Côtes de Castillon, Sainte-Croix-du-Mont, Montagne Saint-Emilion and Canon-Fronsac – you'll be able to spot these on the label.

### WHY THIS WINE?
There's something fun and a bit mischievous about serving one of the world's most renowned red wines with a hamburger – one of the most accessible, democratic and down-to-earth foods there is.

But that's not the only reason to try this pairing. Bordeaux reds are made with Cabernet Sauvignon and Merlot grapes and, depending on which is dominant in your bottle, you'll get a different but equally delicious experience.

Cabernet-led wines have green peppercorn and green pepper notes that are a dream with beef, while Merlot-dominated blends are softer and fruitier with tart, plummy notes that will balance out the richness of the grilled meat.

### IF YOU CAN'T FIND THIS, GO FOR...
A Bordeaux blend from Washington State is an authentically American pairing: the Walla Walla and Columbia Valleys are famous regions to look for.

### IF ALL ELSE FAILS, ASK FOR...
A medium- to full-bodied, well-balanced red wine with lots of complexity.

# Chicken Burger + Sonoma Sauvignon Blanc

WHAT'S THE WINE?

A white wine made in Sonoma County, California, from the Sauvignon Blanc grape. This very versatile grape originated in France's Loire Valley, but the winemakers of California have adopted it and developed their own groundbreaking and brilliant styles of wine. In the Loire, wines made from Sauvignon Blanc are fresh, citrusy numbers, but under the warmer Californian sun you'll get more stone fruit flavours, such as peach and apricot.

WHY THIS WINE?

For this pairing, let's assume you're starting with a classic fast food chicken burger, perhaps from a certain Scottish-sounding burger joint: a breaded, fried fillet of chicken in a soft bun with a good smear of mayonnaise and, crucially, some shredded lettuce that turns from crispy to warm and slightly soggy the longer you take to eat it.

A Sonoma Sauvignon Blanc has more than enough power and body to take on that big slab of protein, while its acidity will cut through the oily mayo and keep your mouth feeling fresh. Finally, the grape's characteristic grassy, green, herbaceous notes will set off the shredded lettuce.

IF YOU CAN'T FIND THIS, GO FOR...

A Sauvignon Blanc from the South of France or the Touraine area of the Loire Valley. A Sauvignon Blanc from New Zealand will work, too.

IF ALL ELSE FAILS, ASK FOR...

A rich, fresh white wine with some herbaceous, green notes.

# Chicken Nuggets + Soave

A white wine from the area around Verona, in Italy, made with a blend of grapes: mostly Garganega, plus some Chardonnay and Trebbiano.

Soave wines are really accessibly priced, so you can have fun experimenting and finding your favourite. Bottles labelled 'Soave Classico' are the next level up in terms of quality and pricing – if you like Soave, you might want to graduate to Soave Classico next time you've got a bit more money burning a hole in your pocket.

WHY THIS WINE?
Chicken nuggets are something of a guilty pleasure; a bottle of Soave makes them doubly so.

These wines have a wonderful richness and texture, which works brilliantly with the chicken and its crispy coating. They also have intriguing, slightly salty, savoury notes, which double down on the moreishness of the nuggets.

IF YOU CAN'T FIND THIS, GO FOR...
A white wine made with the Chardonnay or Chenin Blanc grapes.

IF ALL ELSE FAILS, ASK FOR...
A textured, medium-bodied white wine with some savoury notes.

# Fried Chicken + Manzanilla Sherry

### WHAT'S THE WINE?

A dry fortified wine made in a coastal region in the south of Spain from (mostly) the Palomino grape. Sherry comes in a range of styles, so for this pairing, make sure you get Manzanilla and not, for instance, Amontillado, Oloroso or the dark, sweet Pedro Ximénez (which is great with dessert).

There are a lot of preconceptions around sherry, so put all thoughts of that weird sweet stuff that old people drink at Christmas out of your head and get ready to fall in love with Manzanilla. It's a refreshing, dry and incredibly versatile food wine, and even goes well with tonic instead of a G&T. If you pick up a bottle, you won't regret it.

### WHY THIS WINE?

Fried chicken is such a full-on food – spicy, rich, crunchy and addictive – that it would destroy most wines in your mouth, leaving you barely able to taste them at all.

But sherry is different. Firstly, because it's a fortified wine, it has a higher ABV than regular wines, so it has the power to stand up to punchier food. Secondly, it has a distinctive nutty, savoury flavour – a bit like a dirty martini – that's a great match for the moreishness of fried chicken. Finally, for all its power, Manzanilla sherry has a beautiful freshness. After a few mouthfuls of deliciously greasy fried chicken, you'll be grateful for that.

### IF YOU CAN'T FIND THIS, GO FOR…

A Fino sherry.

### IF ALL ELSE FAILS, ASK FOR…

A nutty, rich and aromatic fortified wine.

# Barbecue Chicken + Ribera del Duero

### WHAT'S THE WINE?

A red wine made by the Duero River in Spain from a blend of grapes including Tempranillo (which is known as Tinto Fino in this part of the world) and aged in oak.

These wines have a labelling system to show how long they've been aged: the word 'Crianza' on the label means the wine's been stored in oak for two years; 'Reserva' means three years, with at least one in oak, and 'Gran Reserva' has been aged for five years, with at least two in oak. Younger wines are more easy-drinking, and cheaper; older wines more complex and pricier. (This system is also used for Rioja wines, so keep an eye out for it there, too.)

### WHY THIS WINE?

Chicken in barbecue glaze is really just a delivery mechanism for that thick sticky sauce based on ketchup, molasses and whatever blend of spices and seasoning your local purveyor of barbecue goodness likes to include. This sauce is the main consideration for wine pairing, as its sweetness will make most wines vanish into a measly nothingness in your mouth.

A Ribera del Duero has plenty of acidity but it also has bold levels of tannins which help break down the food in your mouth and heighten its flavours. Because of the oak ageing, a good Ribera will have incredible chocolate, cinnamon and vanilla notes, plus sticky, dark, dried-fruit flavours, all of which work a treat with the rich molasses-based sauce.

### IF YOU CAN'T FIND THIS, GO FOR...

A Spanish red made from the Mencia grape, a red Rioja, an Italian Super Tuscan or an Australian Shiraz/Syrah.

### IF ALL ELSE FAILS, ASK FOR...

A full-bodied, earthy, rich red wine with plenty of power.

# Fish & Chips + English Blanc de Blancs

## WHAT'S THE WINE?
A dry, sparkling white wine from England made using the same traditional method as Champagne, and the same grapes.

The soil, climate and landscape of the south-east of England, where most of the country's sparkling wine is made, shares key characteristics with the Champagne region of France. Because of this, many pioneers of English winemaking borrowed the style, techniques and even the language of Champagne producers – hence a French term for an English-made wine.

Because production levels are still low, English sparkling wine isn't cheap, but it's more affordable than ever.

## WHY THIS WINE?
There's something very satisfying about pairing a classic English dish with a classic English wine, but there's more to this match than that. We all know that fish and chips is nothing without a sprinkling of vinegar, a good squeeze of lemon, or a gherkin. These are united by acidity, which counteracts the richness of the fish and perks up the chips. English Blanc de Blancs has high levels of acidity, so when you drink it with fish and chips, it has the same effect. Combined with the refreshing effect of bubbles, this is a wine that will cut though the food's glorious greasiness.

The finest bottles of English fizz have a buttery, biscuity flavour – a bit like toasted brioche – which goes particularly well with golden batter and those really crispy chips you find at the bottom of the bag.

## IF YOU CAN'T FIND THIS, GO FOR...
A Blanc de Blancs Champagne would be an ideal alternative.

## IF ALL ELSE FAILS, ASK FOR...
Any dry sparkling white wine made from the Chardonnay grape.

# Reuben Sandwich + Austrian Riesling

## WHAT'S THE WINE?

A white wine made with the Riesling grape in Austria. Neighbouring Germany is much more famous for its Rieslings: the poor old Austrian wines have to live in their shadow and suffer from constant comparisons. However, it's not really helpful to think of these wines as being in competition with each other: they're very different, made in different styles and each with their own merits.

It's worth remembering that Austrian Rieslings can take a bit of time to open up – they need a little air and often a chance to warm up, too. If your wine tastes a bit dull, don't despair: tip it into a jug (don't be too careful as you do this – let the wine splosh about to mix in plenty of air), then pour it rather more carefully back into the bottle, ready to serve. This should wake it up nicely.

One of Austria's best regions for Riesling is Wachau, so look out for that on a label if you can.

## WHY THIS WINE?

A Reuben sandwich is meaty and salty, but also acidic – thanks to the pickles and mustard. Without those garnishes it would be too much to work your way through, but they keep your mouth refreshed so that you come back for another bite. A Riesling works in exactly the same way – bringing some refreshing acidity – while the particularly powerful nature of Austrian wines can stand up to the big flavours of salty, savoury corned beef.

## IF YOU CAN'T FIND THIS, GO FOR...

A German or New World Riesling or a Spanish white made with the Albariño grape.

## IF ALL ELSE FAILS, ASK FOR...

A very ripe white wine with high acidity and big fruit flavours.

# Lamb Doner Kebab + Off-Dry Mosel Riesling

## WHAT'S THE WINE?
A white wine made using the Riesling grape in the Mosel region of Germany. The 'off-dry' bit means that this style of wine has a little bit of sugar in it compared with a dry wine (see p.22). It's not full-on sugary by any means, but it will have just a tiny edge of sweetness to it.

To make sure you're getting a wine at the right level of slight sweetness, look out for the word 'Kabinett' on the label, then aim for an ABV of below 10%. The lower alcohol levels are a sign that not all of the sugar that could have been converted into alcohol has been, so some is left in the wine to add that touch of sweetness.

## WHY THIS WINE?
A doner kebab is – let's not beat about the bush – incredibly rich and fatty: some might even say greasy. That means you need a wine with loads of refreshing acidity that will cut straight through all that richness right away, with enough texture to match up to the full-on nature of a kebab. Mosel Rieslings have both of these things in spades.

Then there's the fact that any decent kebab is loaded with spicy sauces and chillies, so your wine needs to be able to take the heat. That's where the small amounts of sugar in an off-dry Riesling come into their own – they'll balance out the spiciness to perfection.

## IF YOU CAN'T FIND THIS, GO FOR...
A late harvest Riesling from Austria, the New World or the Alsace region of France.

## IF ALL ELSE FAILS, ASK FOR...
An off-dry white wine with high acidity.

# Chicken Shawarma + White Vinho Verde

### WHAT'S THE WINE?
A white wine from the north of Portugal. Confusingly, Vinho Verde means 'green wine', but don't expect something green to come out of the bottle – that's just the name for the region this wine hails from. Historically, wines from this region were always drunk young, and that's what the 'green' in the name refers to. This part of the world makes red, white and rosé wines from a blend of local grapes, but for this pairing we're interested in the whites.

Vinho Verde wines are generally great value for money as they haven't traditionally been much in demand beyond their homeland, although they definitely deserve to be drunk far and wide.

### WHY THIS WINE?
A spicy chicken kebab needs something super refreshing to perk it up and cut through its fattiness. Vinho Verde whites have really high acidity, making them a dream match for food in general (in Portugal you'll often see them served with rich, grilled seafood dishes), but particularly with this dish. A sip of this wine is like squeezing a wedge of lemon over your kebab to liven it up: you'll get a crisp, fresh flavour with notes of ripe yellow apple as well as that citrussy freshness.

### IF YOU CAN'T FIND THIS, GO FOR...
Wine made with the Riesling or Albariño grapes, a Picpoul from France, or an Assyrtiko from Greece.

### IF ALL ELSE FAILS, ASK FOR...
A high-acidity white wine with lots of citrus flavours.

# Vietnamese Noodle Salad + Clare Valley Riesling

### WHAT'S THE WINE?

A white wine made with the Riesling grape in Australia's Clare Valley. Riesling is a classic German grape, but Australia's winemakers have made it their own and now produce some of the finest Rieslings in the world. You can find Rieslings in a range of styles, from dry to sweet. Ideally, for this pairing you want a wine that isn't totally dry, but which has a little sugar in it: look for the words 'late harvest' or 'cordon cut' on the label to identify them.

### WHY THIS WINE?

A Vietnamese noodle salad has a lot going on: fresh green herbs, sliced chilli and crunchy vegetables with bite and texture. Riesling makes such complex, powerful but still drinkable wines that it is more than capable of taking on all that.

The interesting thing about Rieslings grown in Australia, rather than their native, rather cooler Germany, is that they develop ripe tropical fruit flavours – think mango and papaya, then think how beautifully those flavours go together with (and indeed, feature in) Vietnamese food. Rieslings are super aromatic, too, which works like a dream with the fresh green scents of the herbs and the fire of the chilli. If you've found a wine with a little touch of sweetness, that will take the edge off the heat of the chilli even further, all while bringing out their own special fresh flavour.

(You could equally swap a salad for a Banh Mi sandwich here, too.)

### IF YOU CAN'T FIND THIS, GO FOR...

A late harvest Sauvignon Blanc or an off-dry Riesling from either Germany or Austria would work well here.

### IF ALL ELSE FAILS, ASK FOR...

A ripe, refreshing, full-bodied white with residual sugar and good acidity.

# Ramen + Picpoul de Pinet

## WHAT'S THE WINE?

A white wine from the Languedoc, in south-west France: Picpoul is the name of the grape, and Pinet is the area where it's grown.

Picpoul has gone from zero to hero in recent years – from a virtually unknown local wine to a name that now appears on wine lists in restaurants and bars everywhere, and on the shelf of every wine shop or supermarket aisle.

## WHY THIS WINE?

Umami – the 'fifth flavour' (which is translated as something like savoury-ness) – is the essence of a good bowl of ramen, from the intense, rich, silky stock to the eggs and meat often added to the noodles. All those umami flavours need something very zesty and fresh to cut through and keep you feeling refreshed. Picpoul wines have extremely high natural acidity, which makes them ideal here, but they also have plenty of body so they won't be overpowered by the richness of the stock and toppings. You'll notice that the saltiness of the food makes the wine taste a touch sweeter and softer, too.

## IF YOU CAN'T FIND THIS, GO FOR...

Spanish whites made from grapes such as Albariño and Verdejo will give you a similar effect.

## IF ALL ELSE FAILS, ASK FOR...

A full-bodied white wine high in acidity and freshness.

# CHINESE at a glance

Prawn Sesame Toast

Spring Rolls

Salt & Pepper Squid

Sweet & Sour

Chow Mein

Szechuan Sauce

Spare Ribs

Peking Duck

| | | |
|---|---|---|
| Dry Fizz | | Cava<br>Franciacorta<br>Chardonnay |
| Sherry | | Manzanilla<br>Fino |
| Off-Dry White | | Gewürztraminer<br>Pinot Gris<br>Riesling |
| Light-Bodied Red | | Pinot Noir<br>Dolcetto<br>Beaujolais |
| Full-Bodied Red | | South African Shiraz<br>Rhône Blend<br>California Zinfandel |

# INDIAN at a glance

Saag Paneer

Onion Bahji

Papadums & Chutney

Chicken Tikka

Tandoori Chicken

Samosas

Rogan Josh

Zesty & Fresh White

Vinho Verde
Sauvignon Blanc
Muscadet

Off-Dry White

Grüner Veltliner
Pinot Gris
Riesling

Korma

Pink Fizz

Pét Nat
Sparkling New World
Franciacorta

Light-Bodied Red

Gamay
South African Cinsault
Trousseau

Full-Bodied Red

Merlot
Malbec
Sangiovese

# MEXICAN at a glance

Enchiladas

Nachos

Ceviche

Quesadillas

Burritos

Refried Beans

Chilli

Sherry

Fino
Manzanilla

Tacos

Blanc de Blancs Fizz

English Sparkling
Champagne
Crémant

Zesty & Fresh White

Sauvignon Blanc
Riesling
Muscadet

Textured & Rich White

Chenin Blanc
Chardonnay
Semillon

Spicy Red

Tempranillo
Zinfandel
Shiraz

# JAPANESE at a glance

Tempura

Sashimi

Ramen

Sushi

Katsu

Teriyaki

Yakitori

# TRY

| | | |
|---|---|---|
| Dry Fizz | | Cava<br>Franciacorta<br>Chardonnay |
| Blanc de Blancs Fizz | | English Sparkling<br>Champagne<br>Crémant |
| Off-Dry White | | Gewürztraminer<br>Pinot Gris<br>Riesling |
| Light-Bodied Red | | Pinot Noir<br>Beaujolais<br>Valpolicella |
| Full-Bodied Red | | Bordeaux Blend<br>Cabernet Franc<br>Cabernet Sauvignon |

# PIZZA at a glance

Ham & Pineapple

Fiorentina

Margherita

Roasted Veg

Pepperoni

BBQ Chicken

Hot & Spicy

Meat Fest

# TRY

| | |
|---|---|
| Off-Dry White | Pinot Gris<br>Gewürztraminer<br>Riesling |
| Complex White | Soave<br>White Burgundy<br>South African<br>Chenin Blanc |
| Light-Bodied Red | Valpolicella<br>Beaujolais<br>Nebbiolo |
| Medium-Bodied Red | Merlot<br>Barbera<br>Grenache |
| Full-Bodied Red | Aglianico<br>Zinfandel<br>South African<br>Shiraz/Syrah |

# 4

going
the extra
mile

When you're cooking something special – for a special occasion or for special people – the stakes are that bit higher. Fancy food doesn't have to mean fine (i.e. expensive) wine, but the nature of the occasion does call for extra thought.

This chapter will keep your life simple and delicious on a couple of different fronts. If you're the one cooking, you're probably laying on a few bottles of wine, too, to get things going, so of all the things you have to think about, at least choosing the wine can be a doddle.

But that's not even the half of it. What about your guests? 'A bottle' has got to be the most frequent answer to the classic dinner party question: 'Can I bring anything?' When your guests arrive, you're not going to want to look ungrateful by taking said bottle out of their hands at the door ... then never opening it.

But if you're serving steak and they've brought a really light white, or if you've roasted a chicken and they've picked out a heavy red, neither your cooking nor their generosity will be well served by a badly matched food and wine combination. Both the food and the wine will come out of it poorly. So what do you do? Open it anyway? Or look like you're ignoring their gift?

No wonder choosing a bottle of wine under these circumstances can be a fraught experience – especially if you're a guest hoping to impress a host (in-laws, new girlfriend/boyfriend's oldest friends...). It's easy for people to feel under pressure to go for something expensive in these situations, but a wine that's keenly priced but carefully chosen to complement the food will always be a better option.

So, as a host yourself, when guests ask what they can bring, you don't have to stop at just 'a bottle'. You can use this chapter to give them a better steer – no matter how topline – so they don't have to fret about what to buy.

And if you're a guest yourself? Then you have it in your gift to contribute a really well-chosen wine that will take the evening up a notch for everyone around the table – which, after all, is just about the best thing you can offer any host. You might even get invited back.

# Sirloin & Chips + Cahors

## WHAT'S THE WINE?

A French red that takes its name from a region of south-west France, where it's made using the Côt grape. This grape is local to the area but is better known as Malbec – the name it goes by when grown in other parts of the world. Because of this, some winemakers from Cahors are labelling their wines with that better-known name, so keep an eye out for both.

## WHY THIS WINE?

We tend to think of steak as a punchy, even macho, dish, so it's easy to assume that you'd want a really big-shot red to go with it. But cuts of beef vary hugely, and sirloin isn't particularly high in fat compared with other parts of the animal: a high fat content is what demands the biggest hitters of the wine world, and that's just not where we are with sirloin. Anything too powerful on the wine front would drown it out, and when you've spent time and money on a brilliant slab of beef, just as you wouldn't ruin it by cooking it until it's grey, you don't want to overwhelm it with a red that has too many tannins, or is too acidic.

Cahors is bold and full-bodied enough to wash down an intensely savoury, slightly bloody steak, thanks to its inky, plummy flavours of dark fruit and berries, but it has soft, balanced tannins and gentle layers of acidity that won't shout over the meat.

## IF YOU CAN'T FIND THIS, GO FOR…

An Argentinian Malbec, a red wine from the south-west of France, Grenache-/Garnacha-based wines, or Tuscan reds.

## IF ALL ELSE FAILS, ASK FOR…

A medium- to full-bodied red wine with good amounts of tannin and acidity that will give you black fruit flavours such as blueberries, plums and blackberries, plus notes of spice.

# Beef Wellington + Willamette Valley Pinot Noir

## WHAT'S THE WINE?

A red wine made from the Pinot Noir grape that's produced in Willamette Valley, Oregon.

## WHY THIS WINE?

Beef Wellington is a balancing act between buttery golden pastry, earthy mushrooms and that beautiful pink beef all wrapped up in the middle. It's the beef that should always be the star of the show, but it's important to remember that the cut used in a Wellington – a fillet – is the leanest there is, and very subtle in flavour compared with other fattier and more intensely flavoured parts of the animal. This means you need a red wine that won't overpower the tender flavours of the beef, but that can still stand up to the intensity and richness of everything else on your plate.

A Willamette Pinot Noir toes that exact line: these wines have intensity, power and lots of bright red fruit flavours, as well as their own slight earthiness – a characteristic of the Pinot Noir grape – to go with the mushrooms. But they're not nearly as heavy as many other reds, so your fillet will still shine through.

## IF YOU CAN'T FIND THIS, GO FOR...

A Sonoma Pinot Noir from California, or one from Geelong in Australia.

## IF ALL ELSE FAILS, ASK FOR...

A medium- to light-bodied red wine that has good fruit structure but that isn't in-your-face fruity, with smooth tannins.

# Venison + Piemonte Barbera

## WHAT'S THE WINE?

A red wine from the Piedmont region of Italy (called Piemonte in Italian, and therefore written as such on most labels) made with the region's typical Barbera grape. These wines are less fashionable than some other Italian reds, so you can pick them up for relatively bargainous prices.

## WHY THIS WINE?

Venison is an unusual meat: deliciously dark and gamey with an unmistakable intense flavour, but also extremely lean, with barely any fat to speak of. It's also seasonal, so you'll probably be eating it during the depths of autumn and winter, served with fruity sauces and hearty accompaniments.

To go with dark but lean meat and all those trimmings, you want a dark, lean wine: a red that has lots of fruit flavours and isn't too full-bodied but can still warm you up on a winter's day. Piemonte Barbera wines combine a lovely freshness with dark fruit flavours – think blackberry, dark cherry and plum – that are perfect with venison.

## IF YOU CAN'T FIND THIS, GO FOR…

From the same region, wines made with the Dolcetto grape would also work. You could also try a wine from the Northern Rhône made with the Syrah grape, or a Californian Pinot Noir.

## IF ALL ELSE FAILS, ASK FOR…

A medium-bodied red wine with low tannins and high acidity.

# Pork Chop + Orange Wine

### WHAT'S THE WINE?

Orange wines are white wines made as if they were reds – see p.16 for more info if you're not familiar with this relatively unusual style of wine.

Orange wines are now being made all over the world, but their heartland is south-eastern Europe – Slovenia and north-east Italy are two major producers of this ancient style of wine.

### WHY THIS WINE?

A proper chop is a thing of heft and beauty: a thick slab of meat with plenty of fat on it, ideally generously salted and grilled over a good heat so the fat reaches that magic point between crispy and melt-in-the-mouth. All in all, this cut of meat is no wallflower, so it needs a punchy wine, and the body and richness of an orange wine is ideal. The tannins in the wine achieved via skin contact mellow out the fat of the chop in a way that a regular white wine just couldn't. On the flavour front, while orange wines do vary a lot, many of the best have gorgeous sage and herbal notes that make perfect partners for pork.

### IF YOU CAN'T FIND THIS, GO FOR...

A wine made from Riesling or Chenin Blanc grapes will also work well.

### IF ALL ELSE FAILS, ASK FOR...

A zesty, fresh full-bodied white.

# Duck + Northern Rhône Syrah

### WHAT'S THE WINE?

A red from the French winegrowing region of the Northern Rhône, made with the Syrah/Shiraz grape, which originated in (or at least very near) this part of the world. This region makes amazing wines but they don't command the same astronomical prices as Bordeaux and Burgundy, so there are far more bargains to be had.

### WHY THIS WINE?

Because duck is such a rich, dark, almost gamey bird, it can stand up to strong flavours – that's why we usually eat it with intensely flavoured spiced or fruity sauces. Think old-school duck à l'orange (can we have a comeback, please?), roast duck with sauces of plum and star anise, or even Peking duck with its glossy, spiced, sweet-yet-salty sauce. The exact same thinking lies behind this choice of wine: the Syrah grape makes wines with a hint of ripe plum flavour and a subtle spiciness.

Wines from the Northern Rhône also very full-bodied: they pack a proper mouthful that can happily take on the intensity and richness of duck in all its crispy-skinned glory.

(It's worth noting that the super-traditional classical wine pairing with duck is a Burgundy Pinot Noir, but as mentioned above, these don't come cheap – so not only will this alternative taste great, it should save you a few pennies.)

### IF YOU CAN'T FIND THIS, GO FOR…

Any wine from the Côtes du Rhône region: this will get you a Syrah-based wine from somewhere in the Rhône Valley, so close enough.

### IF ALL ELSE FAILS, ASK FOR…

A medium-bodied, well-rounded wine, ideally with plums or a plummy flavour listed in the tasting notes.

# Roast Goose + Blaufränkisch

### WHAT'S THE WINE?
A red wine from Austria, made from the Blaufränkisch grape.

Austria produces some of the finest and most underrated wines in Europe but they're all too often overlooked in favour of the big guns in neighbouring Germany and Italy. Blaufränkisch is one of the country's most celebrated red wine grapes.

Austrian winemakers won't always put the name of the grape on their labels, so look out for the name Burgenland – the region in Austria where this grape is commonly grown.

### WHY THIS WINE?
Goose is an outrageously rich winter treat – dense, dark, with masses of delicious golden fat that melts out as you roast it. The richness of goose dictates the foods we eat with it – sharp, tangy accompaniments to cut through, such as puréed apples or red cabbage with vinegar and spices. This thinking also shapes the best choice of wine.

The bold red fruit flavours in an Austrian Blaufränkisch work much like the fruity sauces and sides you'll often find served with goose – they brighten and cut through the meat. The grape's delicate spiciness echoes the flavours of the spiced red cabbage that goes so well with this bird and should warm you up deliciously on a dark midwinter night.

There's another reason why goose and Austrian wine are a perfect combination. Goose is a big deal in Austria, where it's eaten every autumn with red cabbage and potatoes to mark the feast of Saint Martin – who also happens to be the patron saint of winemakers.

Legend has it that the saint's hiding place was given away one night by the honking of geese in the stable where he was sheltering. The unarguable

Austrian logic goes that there's no better revenge to take on those thoughtless geese than roasting and eating their fellow birds.

**IF YOU CAN'T FIND THIS, GO FOR...**
Wines made from the Zweigelt grape (related to Blaufränkisch) or most Austrian reds.

**IF ALL ELSE FAILS, ASK FOR...**
A red wine with good structure and acidity, soft fruit and low to medium levels of tannins.

# Roast Pheasant + English Pinot Noir

### WHAT'S THE WINE?

A red wine made in England from the Pinot Noir grape. English wines are best known in their Champagne-style sparkling form, but there are some delicious reds now being produced in Sussex, Hampshire and Kent, and this grape is well suited to the relatively cool climate.

These wines are best slightly chilled: conveniently, pheasant is in season from October to February, so you can stick the bottle outside for an hour before bringing it back into the warmth to wash down with your dinner.

### WHY THIS WINE?

Pheasant is a food with a real watch-out: getting the pairing wrong won't just reduce the enjoyment of your meal, it could ruin it. This bird's distinctive flavour will turn into a genuinely unpleasant metallic sensation in your mouth if you eat it with a wine that's high in tannins. To avoid such disasters, look for a light-bodied wine (meaning not too tannic), which makes Pinot Noir (particularly English Pinot Noir) a great option.

What's more, pheasant, and all the tradition of the game shoot – tweed, hipflasks, misty damp countryside, feels so incredibly English that it just seems right to match it with an English wine, in mood as well as in flavour. The best English Pinot Noirs have dark, fruity, blackcurrant and berry flavours – echoes of autumn hedgerows in your glass to drink with this wild bird.

### IF YOU CAN'T FIND THIS, GO FOR…

A Pinot Noir from the Burgundy or Alsace regions of France, or a German Pinot Noir (here, the grape is known as Spätburgunder) or wines from the Valpolicella region of Italy – but not wines labelled 'Ripasso di Valpolicella', which will be too intense to drink with pheasant.

### IF ALL ELSE FAILS, ASK FOR…

A light-bodied red wine with low tannins and tart red fruit flavours.

# Cured or Smoked Salmon + German Riesling

### WHAT'S THE WINE?

A white wine from Germany made with Riesling grapes. But wait! you might cry. Aren't German wines really sweet? Well, no – not the dry ones...

It's true that many German wines exported in the past were pretty sweet, but only because that was the fashion for wines a few decades ago. The versatile Riesling grape can make wines in every style, from bitingly bone-dry to – yes – sweet dessert wines, and everything in between. It's definitely the dry kind you want with your salmon, though.

The German wine classifying system is, it must be admitted, probably the most complicated in the world, and laced with long and hard-to-pronounce words to boot. But you don't need to get your head round that to get hold of the right kind of wine: just look for the word 'trocken' (German for dry) or 'Kabinett' (a specific style of dry wine) on the label.

### WHY THIS WINE?

Whether you're serving it sliced, plain and simple, as a first course, in a mousse, or in a canapé, we all instinctively know that the oiliness and intensity of salmon benefits from a good dash of acidity – usually a squeeze of lemon. The same thing goes for drinking with it: you want a wine with plenty of really fresh, citrusy acidity to cut through and stand up to the flavour.

The best German Rieslings offer all this, plus crisp, green apple flavours and lots of texture in the mouth – again, ideal with such a rich food.

### IF YOU CAN'T FIND THIS, GO FOR...

Riesling from the Alsace region of France or a Riesling from New York – the upstate Finger Lakes region makes particularly great wines.

### IF ALL ELSE FAILS, ASK FOR...

A dry, unoaked white wine that's super fresh and full of acidity.

# Whole Roast Celeriac + White Rhône Blend

## WHAT'S THE WINE?

A white wine from the Rhône region of France – a place where winemakers are experimenting with different grapes, blends and styles. Look out for the words 'Rhône Blanc' on the front of the label, as well as the more specific winegrowing areas of Condrieu, Château-Grillet or Saint-Joseph.

Some of the grapes used here are rarely grown anywhere else in the world – Marsanne, Roussanne, Ugni Blanc and Clairette are some of the unusual ones, while you might have heard of Viognier. With celeriac, check the label to find a wine with a high percentage of Viognier.

## WHY THIS WINE?

Celeriac may not have much going for it in the looks department, but its earthy, fragrant flavour and its versatility – roast whole for a stand-out vegetarian main, mashed or in a soup – make it an autumn and winter favourite. The southern Rhône is a warm part of the world, meaning the grapes get super ripe, which in turn leads to really richly flavoured and textured wines: ideal with this complex vegetable.

Rhône blends also aren't very acidic, which would make your celeriac taste watery and flat. What they do offer are very elegant floral notes that will make the perfect partner for the ugly, earthy, but ultimately lovable celeriac: a true beauty and the beast combo, if ever there was one.

## IF YOU CAN'T FIND THIS, GO FOR…

A white wine from the south of Burgundy more generally, including the Mâconnais; a white wine from France's Rhône Valley, or a wine made from the Viognier grape.

## IF ALL ELSE FAILS, ASK FOR…

A well-rounded, aromatic white wine with lots of texture.

# Salmon en Croûte + Crémant de Bourgogne

### WHAT'S THE WINE?

Sparkling white wine from the Burgundy region of France: 'crémant' is just French for fizzy. Of course, the most famous fizzy wine in the world is French – Champagne. But only wines from the Champagne region get this name; other parts of France also produce delicious and, yes, much cheaper sparkling wine, known as crémants.

Many Burgundian crémants are made from Chardonnay and Pinot Blanc grapes, which you'll also find in a lot of Champagnes – but you're not paying for the Champagne 'brand' or flashy marketing, so arguably you get a lot more bang for your buck.

Look out for the word 'Eminent' on the label, too: it tells you the wine has been aged for at least 24 months to give it a fuller feel in your mouth, plus extra toasty, buttery notes that will work well here.

### WHY THIS WINE?

Salmon en croûte is an indulgent way to serve what is already one of the richest fish there is, surrounding it in a layer of buttery pastry that would overwhelm more delicate flavours. The traditional accompaniment of creamy green watercress sauce, with a good squeeze of lemon, goes some way to cut through that richness, but you'll need your wine to do some of the work, too.

A Burgundian crémant combines refreshing green apple and citrus flavours that will lift and showcase the fish, plus a rich, buttery fullness that will complement the golden pastry.

### IF YOU CAN'T FIND THIS, GO FOR...

Crémant d'Alsace (Alsace is another region of France that also makes great fizz), a good-quality Cava, or any crémant in general. Don't substitute Prosecco – although it's fizzy, it's made in a totally different way from

Champagne/crémant/Cava, so it has a totally different flavour profile and feel in the mouth.

## IF ALL ELSE FAILS, ASK FOR...

Cava and crémants are very widely available sparkling wines, but if you're really stuck, a still white wine with lots of texture and body, ideally made with the Chardonnay grape, will work too – although you won't get quite the same experience.

# ROASTS at a glance

Turkey

Chicken

Pork

Nut Roast

Lamb

Beef

Zesty & Fresh White

Albariño
Riesling

Textured White

Chardonnay
Chenin Blanc
Jura White

Light-Bodied Red

Pinot Noir
Poulsard
Pineau d'Aunis

Full-Bodied Red

Malbec
Red Bordeaux
California Zinfandel

Spicy Red

Tempranillo
Châteauneuf-du-Pape
Australian
Shiraz/Syrah

# FISH at a glance

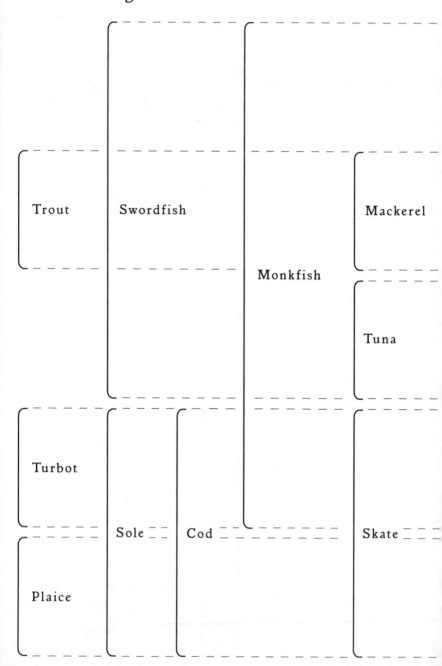

Trout

Swordfish

Mackerel

Monkfish

Tuna

Turbot

Sole

Cod

Skate

Plaice

Light-Bodied Red

Pinot Noir
Beaujolais Nouveau
Valpolicella Classico

Powerful & Fresh White

Riesling
Albariño
Loire Sauvignon Blanc

Oily & Complex White

Soave
Fiano
Viognier

Salmon

Buttery Rich White

Chardonnay
Californian
Sauvignon Blanc
South African
Chenin Blanc

Well-Rounded White

White Burgundy
Sicilian White
White Rioja

5

# snacks and nibbles

Here are wines for all the little moments when a proper feed isn't called for but you still want to nibble – and sip – something.

That could be a light meal when there's only yourself to feed and you don't have the time or energy to make anything more complicated than something tasty on toast. It could be a late-night fridge raid when hunger strikes far outside the usual mealtimes. It could be something small served before a meal to take the edge off everyone's appetite. It could be nibbles laid out at a party to stop everyone getting too drunk too quickly. Or it could be something that will sit on the table within easy reach for dipping into as you settle onto the sofa with a box set.

Whichever it is, if you fancy a glass of wine at the same time, arguably the less substantial the snack, the more important the wine. It becomes much harder to say whether you're eating with your drink or drinking with what you're eating – food and wine have equal importance when the food is only a little something.

There's a long history of drinking accompanied by light mouthful of something tasty in most traditional winemaking cultures – from Spain's tapas to France's apéritif and the Italian aperitivo, and these traditions have evolved for a reason. They're born out of the understanding that by adding a thoughtfully chosen glass of wine to a bite in between meals you can transform a snack from a forgettable, functional refuelling stop to an opportunity to slow down, pause and savour.

# Olives & Nuts + Cava

### WHAT'S THE WINE?
A white sparkling wine from Spain, once known as the 'Spanish Champagne' – although the French cracked down on that pretty hard to protect their own wine. What is still true is that Cava is made using the same method as Champagne and can have much of the same complexity and qualities as the more expensive French fizz, but it's made from different grapes – Macabeo, Parellada and Xarel-lo, to be specific.

### WHY THIS WINE?
Just like Champagne, Cava is incredibly versatile when it comes to pairing it with food. It's got enough body and texture to take on almost anything.

This combination works particularly well not just because of the flavours involved but because of the situations in which you might want to serve both the food and the wine. Snacks and nibbles like olives and nuts are great to have on the table at a party or before the start of a meal, and a glass of bubbles is always going to be the best way to welcome guests.

Traditionally, in Spain, Cava is served in exactly this way, with snacks and nibbles – and with good reason. In this case, the saltiness of both the nuts and the olives will make the wine taste extra refreshing, while Cava's bubbles make a great palate-cleanser – especially useful if you're about to serve more food.

### IF YOU CAN'T FIND THIS, GO FOR...
A Crémant d'Alsace from France if you're on a budget, or Champagne if you've got a reason to splurge.

### IF ALL ELSE FAILS, ASK FOR...
A rich, complex, sparkling, dry white wine.

# Padrón Peppers + Albariño

## WHAT'S THE WINE?

A white wine made with the Albariño (Spanish)/Alvarinho (Portuguese) grape – it's widely planted in the wet, lush, north-west Spanish region of Galicia, near the Atlantic Ocean, as well as in parts of Portugal. This grape makes beautifully aromatic, fresh wines, which is why it's sometimes referred to as the Spanish Riesling – stick your nose in your glass and you'll immediately experience Albariño's beautiful scent.

## WHY THIS WINE?

Padrón peppers are one of Spain's most iconic snacks. They're named after the town of Padrón, which is also found in Galicia, so, as is so often the case, what grows together goes together. These little green peppers are mild nine times out of ten, with bright grassy flavours enhanced by the oil, salt and heat. Albariño's own slightly salty, ocean-breeze tang and herbaceous notes will take those simple but addictive flavours to the next level.

And as for the one in ten peppers that's full-on spicy? Aromatic wines like Albariño are great at helping your mouth cope with heat.

## IF YOU CAN'T FIND THIS, GO FOR...

White wines from France's Alsace region will be in a similar fragrant style: look for ones made with the Pinot Blanc or Gewürztraminer grape, which will bring a sweetness to temper the heat of the peppers.

## IF ALL ELSE FAILS, ASK FOR...

An aromatic, fragrant and fresh white wine.

# Bombay Mix + Sekt Riesling

### WHAT'S THE WINE?

A white sparkling wine from Germany or Austria. 'Sekt' is just the German word for sparkling wine, so it covers a huge range of styles, and the quality can really vary, although a concerted effort is under way to improve standards. The results are impressive. Word hasn't got out much yet, though, meaning these wines are much cheaper than better-known sparkling wines such as Champagne, so you can pick up a real bargain.

Although all kinds of grape can be used to make Sekt, for this pairing, look for a wine made with the Riesling grape.

### WHY THIS WINE?

Bombay mix is all about the spice, and Riesling – be it in still or sparkling wines – is always a great choice for spicy food. The aromatic, perfumed qualities of the wine will help you cope with the heat in your mouth, while the bubbles will keep your palate refreshed. Rather like the way lager and salty snacks go together so well (but even more delicious), each keeps you wanting another sip or bite of the other.

### IF YOU CAN'T FIND THIS, GO FOR…

Crémant d'Alsace – a sparkling wine from France – or an English sparkling wine. If you're feeling fly, a Blanc de Blanc Champagne will work well too.

### IF ALL ELSE FAILS, ASK FOR…

A highly perfumed and aromatic, sparkling, dry white wine.

# Cheese Puffs + Lambrusco

### WHAT'S THE WINE?

A sparkling red wine made in Italy from the Lambrusco family of grapes. But wait – sparkling red? Yes, it's a thing, and it's delicious – plus it's a great talking point. If you've got vague memories of sickly sweet Lambrusco, don't let that put you off either: these can be quality wines, and the best versions are either dry or off-dry. Look for 'secco' or 'semisecco' on the label to ensure you're getting your hands on one of those.

These wines are made in a range of Italian regions and are labelled accordingly, so if you see something marked 'Lambrusco di Modena', for example, it just means the wine was made near the city of Modena.

Lambrusco is best drunk slightly chilled: give it 30 minutes in the fridge before serving.

### WHY THIS WINE?

When you were little, a bowl of cheesy snacks and a can of pop was pretty much the dream. This is the grown-up version and a great combination to serve at a party, not least because of the reactions and conversations that a relatively unknown wine tends to spark.

Lambrusco is a wonderful wine, but it's not a serious wine – it's designed to be drunk outside, in the sun, with snacks and gossip. Its lovely soft, fruity flavours – strawberry, blackberry and rhubarb – work surprisingly well with the saltiness of the cheese puffs, while its gentle fizz will keep you feeling refreshed no matter how many of them you've scarfed.

### IF YOU CAN'T FIND THIS, GO FOR...

A sparkling Aussie red would go down a treat.

### IF ALL ELSE FAILS, ASK FOR...

A sparkling red wine that's easy to drink.

# Popcorn + Montrachet

### WHAT'S THE WINE?

A French white wine from the part of Burgundy called Montrachet, made using the Chardonnay grape. This is a famous wine, so it's easy to find, but not necessarily the cheapest. If you've got a date night in and want to impress, this is the wine to pour as you settle down on the sofa.

You don't want to hide the complexities of this wine, so store it out of the fridge, then put it in for an hour before drinking: it'll be just chilled enough. And serve it in the biggest wine glasses you own (unless you've got one of those novelty ones that holds a whole bottle…) so you can properly appreciate everything it's got going on.

### WHY THIS WINE?

Do you like your popcorn plain, salty or sweet? Whichever you prefer, you'll get a different experience out of your wine. With the plain popcorn, you'll find the Montrachet will taste rich and buttery – you could be forgiven for thinking you'd accidentally eaten buttered popcorn instead. Sipped alongside salted popcorn, the wine will taste sweeter, and you'll get beautiful lemon and green apple flavours. Finally, with a mouthful of sweet popcorn the Montrachet will taste very fresh, and even slightly salty. The vanilla notes that come from the oak barrels it's aged in will also become much more apparent.

Three wines in one? Even a pricier bottle starts to feel like a bargain when you think of it this way…

### IF YOU CAN'T FIND THIS, GO FOR…

Most white wines from Burgundy will do the job, and there are excellent Chardonnays from cooler parts of the New World, too: try something from the Anderson Valley in northern California, or from Tasmania.

### IF ALL ELSE FAILS, ASK FOR…

A textured, rich and well-balanced white wine.

# Scampi Fries + Muscadet

### WHAT'S THE WINE?

A white wine from Muscadet, in France's Loire Valley. Muscadet wines are made using a grape that goes by the spectacularly confusing name of Melon de Bourgogne. It's not a melon and, if used to make Muscadet, won't have been grown in Bourgogne either – Bourgogne, or Burgundy, is a totally different part of France that just happens to be where this grape variety was first grown.

Muscadet is also a brilliantly affordable wine relative to many other French classics, so you can pick up excellent vintage bottles at bargainous prices.

It's easily done, but don't confuse Muscadet with Muscat, which is a grape used to make a very different and often sweet style of wine that's good with dessert.

### WHY THIS WINE?

The locals of the Loire Valley love to drink their Muscadet with oysters and other fishy treats: its refreshing, citrussy flavours and beautiful, slightly salty minerality make it the perfect match for anything that tastes of the sea ... even Scampi Fries. You could also try it with little fried fish, such as whitebait, salt cod or fish croquettes, or, of course, oysters.

### IF YOU CAN'T FIND THIS, GO FOR...

A Picpoul de Pinet or a young Chablis, both from France, or any wine made with the Sauvignon Blanc grape.

### IF ALL ELSE FAILS, ASK FOR...

A lean, dry, citrus-led white wine with good minerality.

# Pork Scratchings + Vouvray

**WHAT'S THE WINE?**
A white wine from the Vouvray part of the Loire Valley, in France, made with the Chenin Blanc grape. Vouvray is often said to be the best wine in the world to use this grape.

Vouvray can be made in a whole range of styles – from dry to sweet, still to sparkling. Often a winemaker will be guided by the weather and conditions that year to decide which type of wine will make the most of his or her crop.

**WHY THIS WINE?**
Whichever style of Vouvray you go for, the same underlying principles mean it's a match made in heaven for fatty, crunchy, salty scratchings. We all know that pork and apples are a dream combo, and Vouvray is famous for making wines with yellow-apple flavours. You'll also get a little ginger or quince flavour in some bottles – both complement pork beautifully.

When it comes to deciding between the different styles of Vouvray, you can let your mood guide you. If you want something super refreshing, look out for a sparkling Vouvray with its bright bubbles. If you want to tone down the saltiness of the scratchings, a slightly sweeter wine will balance that out. If you want a very fresh, clean flavour to contrast with the richness of your snacks, get a still, dry example.

**IF YOU CAN'T FIND THIS, GO FOR…**
A Chenin Blanc from South Africa, the US or other parts of the Loire Valley.

**IF ALL ELSE FAILS, ASK FOR…**
A medium-bodied white wine with lots of vibrant pear and apple flavours, and perhaps a tiny touch of sweetness. Sparkling or still is up to you.

# Jerky/Biltong + South African Pinotage

## WHAT'S THE WINE?

A red wine made in South Africa from the Pinotage grape. This grape is South Africa's gift to the world: it was created there by crossing Cinsault and Pinot Noir in a university lab back in 1924 to make a vine that would give high yields of top-quality grapes.

As with anything, wine has its fashions, and Pinotage was all the rage – and heavily marketed – in the early 2000s. However, it became a victim of its own success, as the race to produce more and more wine led to corners being cut and quality tumbling. For this reason, Pinotage still has a less than brilliant reputation, but since then talented and committed winemakers have gone back to treating the grape properly and producing beautiful wines. Even better, because of that fall from grace, top-notch Pinotage wines are extremely affordable.

## WHY THIS WINE?

'Local is lekker' ('local is delicious') as the South Africans would say. They love this combination of two of their favourite things – dried meat and local wine – so much that they even have an annual Pinotage and Biltong festival. You may not want to go to quite such extremes to celebrate how well this pairing works, but it is undeniably magic. The salty, chewy, super-savoury meat tastes so much more palatable thanks to the blackberry and plum flavours in the wine, while the flavour of the meat will help you identify some of Pinotage's unique tar and bacon flavours. Yes, really.

## IF YOU CAN'T FIND THIS, GO FOR…

A Californian Syrah/Shiraz – look out for one from the Santa Rita Hills. A Spanish red made from the Monastrell grape would also work well.

## IF ALL ELSE FAILS, ASK FOR…

A juicy, medium-bodied red wine with dark red fruit flavours.

# Cured Meat/Charcuterie + Chinon

## WHAT'S THE WINE?

A French red wine from around the town of Chinon, in the region of Touraine, which is located in the Loire Valley. This part of the world, with its cooler climate, is best known for its white wines, so this is a rare red star. A blend of grapes is used: mostly Cabernet Franc, with up to 10 percent of Cabernet Sauvignon permitted.

It's up to you, but a lot of people prefer to drink Chinon slightly chilled. Try it after 30 minutes in the fridge and also at room temperature, then decide which side of the fence you fall on.

## WHY THIS WINE?

Cured meats and charcuterie are pure protein and fat, so they need a wine with good levels of tannins to complement them. Beyond that, a Chinon also has spice and herbal notes to it that will work beautifully with the meat, just as some charcuterie is cured with herbs and spices to give it extra interest.

Finally, this wine has plenty of red fruit flavours, but because the grapes are grown in a cooler climate than many reds, these fruit flavours aren't ripe and jammy but fresh and crunchy – like fruit only just ripe enough to enjoy. That makes a great foil for cured meat – think how well it goes with slightly tart chutneys and you'll get the idea.

## IF YOU CAN'T FIND THIS, GO FOR…

Other red wines from the Loire Valley – look for those from Bourgueil, or Touraine more generally.

## IF ALL ELSE FAILS, ASK FOR…

A medium-bodied red wine with crunchy red fruit and delicate spice.

# Sausage Roll + Alsace White

### WHAT'S THE WINE?

A white wine from the region of Alsace. Today Alsace is part of France, but it was long a contested territory between France and Germany, and was part of Germany for a time, so its wines fall somewhere between French and German styles.

Wines here can be made from a motley mix of different grapes, including Riesling, Pinot Gris, Pinot Blanc, Muscat d'Alsace, Sylvaner and Gewürztraminer, but the most prestigious are generally made from 100 percent Riesling, if your budget can stretch to that.

### WHY THIS WINE?

Alsatian food is heavily influenced by Germany, thanks to its history. There's no nation that loves sausages more than Germany, so it's not surprising to find that Alsatian wines are brilliant with any sausage-based snack. The fresh acidity of the region's white wines cut through the deliciously fatty meat and pastry like a dream.

### IF YOU CAN'T FIND THIS, GO FOR...

A Riesling from Germany, Austria or Australia.

### IF ALL ELSE FAILS, ASK FOR...

A fresh, clean and aromatic white wine.

# Scotch Egg + Colombard

A white wine made from the Colombard grape, most commonly planted in the south of France. This grape can also be used to make brandy, but as brandy has fallen out of favour, Colombard is increasingly being used to make wine instead. Colombard is often blended with other grapes, such as Sauvignon Blanc, but if you can find a 100 percent Colombard, grab it, because it's worth trying in its pure state.

WHY THIS WINE?
Scotch eggs come into their own in two places: pubs and picnics. If you're munching on one in a pub, you're probably washing it down with a beer. But if you're packing up a picnic, you could do a lot worse than to include a bottle of Colombard to pass around. Not only is it a great picnic wine – crisp, aromatic and a great crowd-pleaser – but it works a treat with Scotch eggs.

If Scotch eggs have one flaw, it's that they can be a bit dry, so the fresh hit of lemon you'll get from the wine will make the experience much more palatable, without overpowering the flavour of the egg buried in the middle.

IF YOU CAN'T FIND THIS, GO FOR...
An Italian white made from the Trebbiano grape, or a wine made with Sauvignon Blanc from either the New World (Australia or California) or the warmer south of France.

IF ALL ELSE FAILS, ASK FOR...
A crisp, fresh white wine.

# Potato Waffles + Chilean Carménère

### WHAT'S THE WINE?

A red wine from Chile made from the Carménère grape, which was brought to the country from France in the 1800s and is fast becoming Chile's flagship grape. Some of the very best are made in the region of Colchagua, so keep an eye out for that name on labels.

Oddly, especially given its status and importance in Chile today, Carménère only made it to the country by mistake. It had been confused with Merlot, and the mix-up was only discovered in 1994! Since the grape was later all but wiped out in France by a pest that destroyed vines, this muddle saved Carménère from extinction.

### WHY THIS WINE?

What is absolutely non-negotiable when you're tucking into a plate of nostalgic and comforting hot potato snacks? A big dollop of ketchup, with its sweetness and slight spice and seasoning. Carménère works in exactly the same way, with vibrant, ripe, red fruit flavours coming through on the first mouthful. After a few sips, you'll also taste green pepper notes and a little warm ground pepper, too. Thank goodness for the Merlot muddle: if it hadn't been for that, we wouldn't have this perfect potato partner today.

### IF YOU CAN'T FIND THIS, GO FOR...

A Californian Cabernet Sauvignon from the state's central coast: Ballard Canyon and Santa Rita Hills are names to look out for.

### IF ALL ELSE FAILS, ASK FOR...

A medium- to full-bodied, well-rounded red wine with notes of pepper and good levels of fruit.

# Peanut Butter & Jam Sandwich + Beaujolais

## WHAT'S THE WINE?

A red wine from the Beaujolais region of France, made using the Gamay grape. This region has a long tradition of making very light reds, and they're best served slightly chilled: 30 minutes in the fridge should do the trick. Beaujolais is so light it's really almost like juice, and we all know that juice is best from the fridge – this wine is no different.

Beaujolais wines are meant to be drunk young – within the year – so they're very affordable for the quality.

## WHY THIS WINE?

Beaujolais is soft, fruity and full of strawberry and raspberry flavours ... just like jam. So go easy on the jam if you can bear it, and let the wine do some of the work instead, setting off the rich, salty peanut butter to perfection.

## IF YOU CAN'T FIND THIS, GO FOR...

A red wine made from the Pinot Noir or Zweigelt grapes. Valpolicella Classico, an Italian red, will also work well.

## IF ALL ELSE FAILS, ASK FOR...

A light-bodied, fruity, easy-drinking red.

# Avocado Toast + Sylvaner

A white wine made from the Sylvaner grape, which is grown in Germany and France – particularly the German regions of Franken and Rheinhessen. This was once the most widely grown grape in Germany, before the country fell head over heels for its beloved Riesling.

WHY THIS WINE?
Avocado is a funny one: for all its popularity, nobody could argue that it's got a huge amount of flavour. The pleasure is all in the creamy texture, which makes it such a great foil for other flavours, such as chilli, bacon or salty cheese – whatever you like to add.

That creamy texture is key when it comes to picking a wine, whether you're indulging at brunch or having a simple evening snack. The wine needs to have a lot of texture itself, or it will taste and feel thin and watery against the avocado. Sylvaner has an incredibly rich texture and really coats the inside of your mouth, much like avocado. This wine is also packed with bright green flavours that bring out the freshness of the avocado, and which mean it's equally delicious with asparagus.

IF YOU CAN'T FIND THIS, GO FOR...
Wines made from the Pinot Blanc or Trebbiano grapes.

IF ALL ELSE FAILS, ASK FOR...
A light-bodied white wine with good texture and mouthfeel.

# Pâté on Toast + Bourgogne Red

### WHAT'S THE WINE?

A red wine made with the Pinot Noir grape from the French region of Burgundy ('Bourgogne' in French), but no more precise than that. Some bottles of Burgundy are made from incredibly specific little parcels of land, and these are the wines that command some of the highest prices in the world.

These more generic red Burgundies are affordable, and designed to be drunk young and fresh, unlike their fancy cousins which can, at their best, be aged for years, and which deserve to be drunk with ceremony and on special occasions. But for a tasty snack a simple red Burgundy is just the ticket.

These wines are so fresh and light that they're at their best slightly chilled, so if you remember, put the bottle in the fridge an hour before you want to eat and drink. If you don't remember, no biggie.

### WHY THIS WINE?

Pâté is gamey and rich so it needs something to break it up and cut through it. This means that, like foie gras, it's actually delicious with a sweet dessert wine, but because it's often eaten as a light meal or a starter, let's assume you don't want to drink it with the sort of wine that often rounds off an evening.

Instead, look to other traditional accompaniments to pâté for clues as to what to drink: fruity chutneys, red wine jelly or a little sprig of redcurrants. A fresh red Burgundy has all those tart, barely ripe red fruit flavours and will bring a freshness to what can otherwise be a very intense, rich snack.

### IF YOU CAN'T FIND THIS, GO FOR…

A Beaujolais from France or a Valpolicella Classico from Italy are both lighter-bodied red wines that will also work well here.

### IF ALL ELSE FAILS, ASK FOR…

A light-bodied red wine with crunchy red fruit flavours.

# Cheese Toastie + Merlot

### WHAT'S THE WINE?

A red wine made from the Merlot grape. This is one of the world's great red wine grapes, used to make bargainous table wines as well as some of the most prestigious bottles in the world. Merlot got a bad rep because the market was flooded with poorly made wines but, like all grapes, it all depends on how it's treated, so you can't say you categorically don't like Merlot (or indeed any other single grape) when there's no single way that it can taste. Some of the best and most interesting Merlots in the world are currently being produced in the USA and Chile, as well as in France, where the grape originated, and Italy.

### WHY THIS WINE?

Arguably, the most simple and satisfying of all snacks calls for one of the easiest-drinking wines out there to quaff alongside. You may be a purist and use only cheese and bread, but even if you wouldn't add them in your own late-night fridge-raid snack, you have to admit that ketchup and fruity chutneys are great partners for melted, bubbling golden cheese. Merlot has a similar effect to those, thanks to its warm red fruit flavours. This is also a wine with very soft tannins, which is why it's so easy to drink, but what tannins there are will work perfectly with the rich protein of the cheese to make it even more delicious.

Some Merlots are so light that they're good slightly chilled, meaning you can reach for the wine and the cheese in the fridge in one go. Snacks don't get better than that.

### IF YOU CAN'T FIND THIS, GO FOR...

A red wine made with the Malbec or Cabernet Franc grapes.

### IF ALL ELSE FAILS, ASK FOR...

A medium-bodied, easy-drinking red wine.

# sweet treats

Talking about sweeter foods means it's time to talk about sweet wines. So let's cut right to it: there's a lot of confusion and even snobbery about drinking sweet wines. It's become a kind of point of pride among some people to declare that they only drink dry wines, as if that were proof that they have better taste.

Yet some of the best, most interesting and most exciting wines in the world are made in a sweet style. And when you think about it, it's odd that we're so reluctant to enjoy a little sweetness in our wine. After all, we love sweetness in our food – whether that's the ripe natural sugars of a piece of fresh fruit, or the rather less natural sugars in a piece of cake. And we enjoy sweetness in other drinks, too, from smoothies to cocktails. Even a cappuccino is made more delicious by the naturally occurring sugars in dairy milk.

So don't be shy about leaning into sweeter styles of wine when you're in the mood for something sweet to eat.

But why is it so important?

If you drink a dry wine without much sugar in it while you're eating something sweet, it isn't just that the food and wine won't enhance each other as much as they could. The wine will taste actively bitter, thin and nasty because of the contrast with the food, while the food will lose a lot of its interesting flavours, leaving only a sensation of pure sugariness.

The pairings suggested in this chapter will help you avoid that pitfall, and instead bring out the luscious sweetness of whatever you're treating yourself to.

It should be said that it isn't only sweet foods that can call for a little sweetness in your wine: you'll find recommendations for off-dry (i.e. slightly sweet) wines in other chapters throughout this book.

And, conversely, it isn't always the case that you need to drink a wine with a good touch of sugar if you're eating something sweet, as you'll see … But it's definitely a smart general approach.

There's a whole world of sweet wines out there – white, red, still and sparkling – to try with your favourite desserts and sweet treats.

# Birthday Cake + Moscato d'Asti

### WHAT'S THE WINE?

A lightly sparkling sweet white wine from the Italian region of Piedmont, made near the town of Asti from the Moscato grape (hence the name). This is a low-alcohol wine – typically around 5.5–6% ABV – making it very easy to drink.

### WHY THIS WINE?

A birthday is always cause for celebration, and that means two things (at least for grown-ups): cake and bubbles. That often leads people to think of Champagne – the ultimate in celebratory bubbles – but the problem is that almost all the Champagne you'll be familiar with is made in a dry style, i.e. without very much sugar in it. Match this with a super-sweet birthday cake packed with icing, sprinkles and all the rest, and that expensive Champagne will taste bitter and unpleasant when sipped alongside. What a waste.

For all that, the sentiment is absolutely spot on: the trick is to find a sparkling wine with enough of its own sugar to work well with birthday cake. Moscato d'Asti is perfect in this regard. It isn't only worth loving for its sweetness, though: it has its own incredible scent, with honeysuckle and orange blossom reminiscent of a Mediterranean garden in spring, and it tastes like biting into a ripe peach. The bubbles and the acidity will cut through the rich frosting, ensuring you've got space for another bite…

### IF YOU CAN'T FIND THIS GO FOR…

Another sweet sparkling wine. Look out for words on the label that will tell you that the wine is on the sweet side – this may be 'demi-sec' or 'doux' if they're French; 'amabile' or 'dolce' if they're Italian. You can even get sweet Champagnes, but they're not very fashionable these days and, therefore, very hard to find.

### IF ALL ELSE FAILS, ASK FOR…

A sweet sparkling wine with good amounts of residual sugar.

# Pineapple Upside-Down Cake + Tokaji Aszú

## WHAT'S THE WINE?

A sweet white wine from the Hungarian winegrowing region of Tokaji (pronounced 'tok-eye'), whose wines are so important to Hungarians that they're even mentioned in the country's national anthem.

The Tokaji region produces wines in a range of styles, from dry to super sweet, but it's best known for the latter, which are some of the finest and most highly sought after dessert wines in the world: Aszú is a specific, and very historic, sweet style of Tokaji winemaking.

If you spot the word 'Puttonyos' on labels, it refers to the system used by Hungarians to measure a wine's sweetness. There's no need to master this archaic system, but it's worth noting that a wine labelled 5 Puttonyos is 20 percent sweeter than Coca-Cola.

## WHY THIS WINE?

This is a pairing where the wine and the food mirror each other – to a quite astonishing degree. Sweet wines made using the method employed in Tokaji develop incredibly convincing tropical fruit notes, with flavours almost exactly like those slices of candied mango, papaya and pineapple you can buy in health food stores that trick you into thinking you're eating something healthy. This will make that tinned pineapple on top (or is it the bottom?) of your cake sing. What's more, this wine still retains lots of freshness and acidity – more like a fresh pineapple this time – so it will stop you feeling overwhelmed by the sweetness of the cake itself.

## IF YOU CAN'T FIND THIS, GO FOR...

A Sauternes or Jurançon wine from France, or a sweet late harvest Sauvignon Blanc from Australia.

## IF ALL ELSE FAILS, ASK FOR...

A sweet wine with good acidity and plenty of rich tropical fruit notes.

# Lemon Meringue Pie + Canadian Ice Wine

## WHAT'S THE WINE?

A sweet white wine from Canada, usually produced in Ontario, British Columbia and Nova Scotia, with a beautiful golden hue.

Ice wine is such a romantic term, but it's also completely literal: the winemakers leave the grapes on the vines late into the winter so that the fruit freezes. This concentrates the sugars, and they can then be quickly pressed to make a super-sweet wine.

The other main producer of ice wine is Germany, where it's called Eiswien, but the Canadian versions tend to be much more affordable.

## WHY THIS WINE?

Some sweet wines have tropical fruit or pear flavours, but ice wines have amazing fresh, citrussy flavours – think lemon curd, or marmalade – plus a silky texture that coats your tongue beautifully. This will go perfectly with the creamy curd, while the acidity in the wine will cut through the unadulterated sweetness of the meringue topping.

## IF YOU CAN'T FIND THIS, GO FOR...

Look for a late harvest Australian wine instead.

## IF ALL ELSE FAILS, ASK FOR...

A concentrated sweet white wine with citrus notes.

# Pavlova + Late Harvest NZ Sauvignon Blanc

## WHAT'S THE WINE?

A sweet white wine made in New Zealand from the Sauvignon Blanc grape – a grape the Kiwis are famous for having mastered and made their own. The grapes are harvested in about July, which is the equivalent of December in the Northern Hemisphere – i.e. very, very late – to give them time to become incredibly ripe and sweet.

## WHY THIS WINE?

Pavlova is one of New Zealand's great culinary contributions to the world: it was created there in honour of the ballerina Anna Pavlova, so it feels right to dig into this classic dessert with a wine from the same place.

The key to a good pavlova is the balance between the sweetness of the meringue, the richness of the whipped cream and, crucially, the freshness and acidity of the fruit on top, be that raspberries, passion fruit or – naturally – kiwi fruit.

The same principles are at play here: in a sweet New Zealand Sauvignon you get all the tropical fruit flavours that the grape is known for in dry wines, but they're much more concentrated: passion fruit, sticky honey and pineapple flavours all come through. A well-made sweet wine will still retain its acidity, however, preventing it from becoming sickly, and cutting through the cream and the meringue to perfection.

## IF YOU CAN'T FIND THIS, GO FOR…

A Coteaux du Layon from France, or an Australian late harvest Sauvignon Blanc or Semillon.

## IF ALL ELSE FAILS, ASK FOR…

A floral and tropical late harvest New World wine.

# New York Vanilla Cheesecake
# + Australian Late Harvest Semillon

### WHAT'S THE WINE?

A sweet white wine made in Australia from the Semillon grape. 'Australia' is obviously a pretty broad recommendation, but winemakers here are free to make wines however they like, wherever they are, unlike in other winemaking countries, so there are no set styles by area. The Hunter Valley and Margaret River winegrowing regions are great names to look for on the bottle, though.

'Late harvest' means exactly that – the grapes are left on the vines for as long as possible, which allows them to get extra ripe and sweet. Even a short amount of additional time on the vines can make a big difference to the sweetness of the fruit: think about how much sweeter a banana is after just a few days' ripening in the fruit bowl compared with when you bought it.

### WHY THIS WINE?

A smooth, perfect New York-style cheesecake is hard to improve upon, and messing around with garnishes or sauces only distracts from its pure white simplicity (and deliciousness). The best way to accompany it, therefore, is with something in your glass. These sweet, late harvest wines have complex fruity flavours – you might get a whiff of marmalade, apricot or peach, or even passion fruit. The fresh acidity of the wine will cut through the richness of the cheesecake like a knife, meaning you can eat and eat...

### IF YOU CAN'T FIND THIS, GO FOR...

Try an Aussie late harvest wine made from Sauvignon Blanc instead, or a Coteaux du Layon from France's Loire Valley.

### IF ALL ELSE FAILS, ASK FOR...

A sweet, late harvest New World white wine.

# Vanilla Ice Cream + Pedro Ximénez (PX) Sherry

### WHAT'S THE WINE?
Pedro Ximénez (pronounced 'himenez') is a Spanish grape used to make a specific kind of sweet sherry. For some reason it tends to be referred to by its nickname, PX. Perhaps it just sounds cooler.

Sherry is a fortified wine and PX sherries are some of the sweetest fortified wines in the world: they can be up to four times as sweet as Coca-Cola. Because of all the sugar and extra alcohol, these wines will keep for ages after you've opened the bottle, so it's not too scary an investment to pick one up and try it.

### WHY THIS WINE?
Ice cream is a bit of a bugger to pair with wine. Although it seems like it should be a fun thing to drink with, the fact that it's frozen poses a real problem – chilled taste buds just don't work as well. This is why ice-cream recipes contain a lot more sugar than you'd expect: to ensure your frozen taste buds still have something to taste when you're eating it.

The trick here is to literally combine vanilla ice cream and PX sherry: this isn't so much a pairing as a new way to eat your ice cream. Pour the PX right over the top of a scoop of ice cream – just as you might an espresso, to create an affogato. This makes for the most delicious ice-cream sauce in the world as the two melt together, the wine adding all kinds of complementary flavours to the vanilla, from coffee and dark chocolate, to baked fig, prune and sticky dates. The warmth from the alcohol is the perfect foil for the ice cream. You may never be able to eat ice cream with boring old chocolate or fudge sauce again.

### IF YOU CAN'T FIND THIS, GO FOR...
This pairing only really works with PX, which is such a unique wine. Luckily, it's easier than ever to get your hands on this sherry – be it online or in store.

# Banoffee Pie + Muscat de Rivesaltes

### WHAT'S THE WINE?
A sweet, fortified white wine made in Rivesaltes, in the south of France, using grapes that all belong to the Muscat family. This wine is best served chilled, so be sure to store it in the fridge.

### WHY THIS WINE?
Banoffee pie is an outrageously rich dessert, with sweet thing upon sweet thing and no refreshing or acidic flavours to counteract any of them (unlike, say, a pavlova with its fruit topping). You need a wine that can break through this almost-overwhelming sweetness without being overwhelmed itself. A Rivesaltes is up to that job not just because of its amazingly complex flavours and refreshing acidity, but because of its high alcohol content that can punch through cream and caramel. On the flavour front, it'll add notes of summer fruits and honey to complement the ingredients in the pie.

### IF YOU CAN'T FIND THIS, GO FOR...
Ratafia, a sweet fortified wine produced in France (but also the name given to a herbal, fruity liqueur made in France, Spain and Italy, so check the label to make sure you've got the right one), a Vin Santo from Tuscany, or a Tawny Port.

### IF ALL ELSE FAILS, ASK FOR...
A rich, fortified white wine with honey and fruit flavours.

# Chocolate Tart + Recioto di Valpolicella

## WHAT'S THE WINE?

A top-quality, sweet red wine – far less common, but no less delicious than sweet white wines. This one comes from Italy, from the Valpolicella region of Verona, in the country's north-east, where they also make some of the best dry red wines in the world. As with Vin Santo (see p.145), the sweetness of this wine comes from partially drying the grapes before their juice is extracted, to concentrate their sugars.

## WHY THIS WINE?

A good chocolate tart (or cake) is both super sweet and very intense, especially if it's made with top-quality dark chocolate and lots of cream or butter. That's why we so often serve these desserts with red berries or crème fraîche: the tanginess and acidity of those garnishes cuts through the dense richness of the chocolate.

This wine works in exactly the same way. It's sweet in its own right, which means it won't taste bitter and nasty alongside the sugars in your dessert, but it's got enough acidity to cut through. Because it's a red wine, it also has high levels of tannins to stand up to the rich, dark creaminess of the tart. The one downside of this combination is that you'll feel able to eat far more of a rich dessert than you would without the wine there to help out – or perhaps that's a plus.

## IF YOU CAN'T FIND THIS, GO FOR…

A Ruby Port, or a red Maury or Banyuls from France.

## IF ALL ELSE FAILS, ASK FOR…

A sweet red wine.

# Chocolate Chip Cookies + Sweet Marsala

### WHAT'S THE WINE?

Marsala is what's known as a fortified wine (i.e. it's had extra alcohol added to it) from the Italian island of Sicily, made with three local grapes. It's often found lurking at the back of kitchen shelves because it's used in both sweet and savoury recipes, but few of us tend to think to drink it on its own. That's a shame, because it's delicious.

There are a wide range of styles of Marsala, from dry to sweet; all are worth trying, but for this pairing look for the sweetest one you can find – it's dark amber in colour.

Marsala only gets better with age, so get the oldest one you can afford. Because of the additional alcohol, it will keep much longer once opened than a regular wine, so don't worry about needing to drink it all in one go.

### WHY THIS WINE?

Chocolate is really hard to pair with wine, but Marsala is an exception: this versatile wine loves chocolate – even the strong dark kind. But the wine's own nutty sweetness also works brilliantly with things like caramel. The best sweet Marsalas have a flavour that will remind you of toasted hazelnuts or macadamias, as well as vanilla, muscovado sugar and warm spices, so when you sip it alongside a cookie, it'll taste for all the world like your cookie has chunks of toasted nut and sweet spices in it – even if it's just a bog-standard supermarket biscuit.

### IF YOU CAN'T FIND THIS GO FOR…

The sweet Italian wine known as Vin Santo, Rivesaltes from France, or Oloroso sherry from Spain.

### IF ALL ELSE FAILS, ASK FOR…

Something dark, sweet and nutty – it could even be a liqueur.

# Chocolate Brownies + Red Banyuls

## WHAT'S THE WINE?

A sweet red wine from the south-west French region of Roussillon – specifically, Banyuls – made from the Carignan and Grenache grapes. Its sweetness comes from the addition of extra alcohol during the wine-making process (meaning it counts as a fortified wine), plus the charming practice of storing the wine outside in the sun in giant glass bottles, which concentrates the sugar and the flavours.

Banyuls can taste a lot like port, with which most people are more familiar, but it's much brighter in flavour, with more red fruit notes.

This wine is best served slightly chilled, so pop it into the fridge about 40 minutes before you want to drink it.

## WHY THIS WINE?

It's hard to find fault with chocolate brownies, but if you were really pushed it would be that they can be almost too rich – especially if you're serving them as dessert. Banyuls brings freshness and acidity to the chocolateyness to help it go down more easily, but because the wine is so sweet itself, it won't taste bitter or flat after a mouthful of brownie.

## IF YOU CAN'T FIND THIS, GO FOR…

Port or a red Maury, also from France.

## IF ALL ELSE FAILS, ASK FOR…

A sweet red wine.

# Crêpes + Jurançon

### WHAT'S THE WINE?
A sweet white wine from the Jurançon region in the far south-west of France, made from a blend of grapes. This part of the world makes both sweet and dry wines, so check the label to get the right kind. The sweetness comes from the practice of leaving the grapes on the vines for as long as possible.

### WHY THIS WINE?
We all know instinctively that refreshing citrus fruits work brilliantly with a classic lacy crêpe, be it the home-made lemon and sugar version, or the old-school (but delicious) restaurant classic that is Crêpes Suzette.

In a sweet Jurançon wine you'll find a range of pure, clear fruit flavours of all kinds, including apricot, pineapple and mango, but also a lovely zesty orange hint which keeps the wine fresh and will work beautifully with your pancakes.

### IF YOU CAN'T FIND THIS, GO FOR...
A Barsac from France, an Australian late harvest Semillon, or an off-dry Riesling from Clare Valley in Australia.

### IF ALL ELSE FAILS, ASK FOR...
A late harvest sweet wine with citrus flavours and aromas.

# Sugared or Jam Doughnuts +
# Australian Shiraz / Syrah

## WHAT'S THE WINE?

A red wine made in Australia from the Shiraz/Syrah grape. Australia now makes some of the best Shiraz-based wines in the world: soft, elegant and complex. This grape is widespread across the country, but look for the names Barossa Valley and McLaren Vale on the label for some of the best.

## WHY THIS WINE?

For this pairing, think of a relatively restrained, classic doughnut – not something topped with chocolate and frosting, but a plain sugared doughnut or, even better, a traditional jammy one.

It's that jam that holds the key. Nothing beats biting into a doughnut and hitting the oozing patch of jam hidden within it. An Australian Shiraz brings its own jamminess to the table to make everything twice as fun, thanks to the big fruit flavours of blackberry, strawberry and raspberry that come through even without much sweetness in the wine itself.

Doughnuts are coated in sugar but the dough itself isn't super sweet, so you can drink a dry wine alongside and everything will balance out perfectly.

## IF YOU CAN'T FIND THIS, GO FOR…

Port, a red Banyuls from France, or a Californian Zinfandel.

## IF ALL ELSE FAILS, ASK FOR…

A bold, full-bodied red wine with big black and red fruit flavours.

# Biscuits + Vin Santo

### WHAT'S THE WINE?

Vin Santo means 'holy wine' in Italian, although its religious credentials these days are dubious. It's a sweet, amber-coloured dessert wine made in Tuscany that Italians will often serve at the end of a meal. Its sweetness comes from partially drying the grapes in the sun before extracting the juice, which concentrates the sugars. Think how much sweeter a raisin tastes than a grape and you've got the idea. Wines made this way are called passito wines.

Vin Santo should be served slightly chilled but not cold. Give it 30–45 minutes in the fridge before you serve it.

### WHY THIS WINE?

Italians tend to serve Vin Santo – be it at the end of the meal, or to a guest who's popped round of an afternoon – with biscotti. It's just like offering someone tea and biscuits, or coffee and cake, but much more fun.

Much like a cup of tea, the wine isn't just there to drink alongside the biscuits but to dip them into. The sweet treats will soak up the hazelnut, honey and caramel flavours of the wine and allow everything to dissolve in your mouth in one delicious go.

The best bit is that this works with almost any biscuit, cookie or small cake, such as a madeleine – no matter how ordinary. Yes, even shortbread, or a digestive. You can serve them this way after a meal, or swap out the usual glass of wine and bag of crisps you'd pick up for a night in with a box set.

### IF YOU CAN'T FIND THIS, GO FOR...

This is one of those rare cases where a wine is so unique that it's hard to suggest a substitute. It's worth making the extra effort to find it.

### IF ALL ELSE FAILS, ASK FOR...

A sweet and concentrated complex wine with some nutty flavours.

# HOT PUDDINGS at a glance

Crumble

Pie

Baked Cheesecake

Strudel

Sticky Toffee Pudding

Rice Pudding

| | | |
|---|---|---|
| Sweet & Zesty White | | Chenin Blanc<br>Riesling<br>Recioto di Soave |
| Sweet Tropical White | | Jurançon<br>Sauternes<br>NZ Late Harvest |
| Sweet Rich Red | | Maury<br>Banyuls<br>Red Port |
| Syrupy | | Pedro Ximénez<br>(PX) |
| Fortified | | Port<br>Ratafia |

7

cheese
please

Whether you do things the French way and serve cheese before the dessert course, or the Anglo-Saxon way and serve it as the final course, lazily alternating a nibble of cheese with a sip of wine is a wonderful way to ease yourself towards the end of a meal.

One of the most amazing things about both wine and cheese is that they're both reminders of what different techniques, regions and producers can do with the same simple, basic ingredients – milk and grapes – to create wildly different end products. Exploring those differences, and how they complement each other, is one of the best things about drinking wine with cheese.

Wine and cheese are also both wonderfully sociable things to eat and drink. Sharing a cheeseboard is a great way to get people talking. It goes without saying that a bottle of wine does the same. Whether it's as part of a dinner or at a party, picking a couple of wines that set off a cheese plate brilliantly gives people something to talk to each other about as they try the different combinations.

Finally, it's worth remembering that when you drink the right wine with cheese it will refresh your palate, which makes it easier to keep on nibbling away at something so rich – even if you're several courses deep into a meal. More cheese? That can only be a good thing.

# Goat's Cheese + Sancerre

### WHAT'S THE WINE?

A white wine from Sancerre in France's Loire Valley. Sancerre is made in a range of styles, from red to white to rosé, although white – the most commonly available and best known – is what you want here.

Sancerre white is made from the Sauvignon Blanc grape, which some people have had bad experiences with and so can be wary of. (The phrase 'cat's piss' is often used to describe badly made Sauvignon Blanc wines.) But this grape can make such different wines depending on where it's grown and how it's handled that you shouldn't let bad memories put you off.

### WHY THIS WINE?

It's time to reach for the old adage again: what grows together, goes together. The Loire Valley is famous not only for its wine but for its world-class goat's cheese.

Goat's cheese goes brilliantly with grapes, with beetroot and with citrus. Guess what? All those flavours come through in a Sancerre. There are mineral flavours, too, which work perfectly against the slightly chalky flavour specific to goat's cheese. And because most goat's cheeses are relatively young and mild, the subtle magic of a Sancerre won't overpower them.

### IF YOU CAN'T FIND THIS, GO FOR...

Any white wine from the wider Loire Valley region made from Sauvignon Blanc: look out for the name Touraine (another part of the region) on the label. A Muscadet or young Chablis, both from France, will also work well. Or try a Chilean Sauvignon Blanc: look for one whose label doesn't make a big deal out of it being fruity, as you want something quite restrained.

### IF ALL ELSE FAILS, ASK FOR...

A dry white wine that's fresh, clean and has good levels of aromatics.

# Brie + Blanc de Blancs Champagne

### WHAT'S THE WINE?

Another style of France's most famous wine – this one made entirely with white grapes, hence the name, which means 'white from white'. These wines can be made from a wide variety of grapes, with Chardonnay the most commonly used.

### WHY THIS WINE?

Brie has one of the highest fat contents (mmm) of all the well-known soft cheeses, which calls for a particularly fresh and zippy wine to cut through it and keep your mouth refreshed. Blanc de Blancs Champagnes have all the toasty brioche notes common to every Champagne style, but they're layered here with zingy green apple flavours. If you're lucky (and flush) enough to get your hands on an aged or vintage Champagne, this will also have rich, warm, nutty notes. Brie, apples and walnuts from every bite and sip: it doesn't get much better than that.

### IF YOU CAN'T FIND THIS, GO FOR...

Any dry sparkling wine made in the Blanc de Blancs Champagne style, anywhere in the world; or a 100 percent Chardonnay or Pinot Blanc sparkling wine from France's Alsace region.

### IF ALL ELSE FAILS, ASK FOR...

A sparkling Chardonnay of any sort, or any sparkling white with 'extra brut' on the label – this is a sign that it'll be dry and particularly refreshing.

# Camembert + Blanc de Noirs Champagne

## WHAT'S THE WINE?

A sparkling white wine from the Champagne region of France, but then you probably knew that. Blanc de Noirs is a way of describing Champagne made from red grapes – it literally means 'white from red'. It's made from two grape varieties: Pinot Noir and Pinot Meunier.

No, Champagne isn't cheap. But if you steer clear of the most famous names (where you're paying a lot for the brands, and for the vast marketing budgets put behind them), you can get some bargains. The cost also reflects the complexity of Champagne production, so you're paying for expertise and time.

## WHY THIS WINE?

Champagne is a great way to kick off a party, so if you're serving cheese at a gathering, popping a cork alongside declares the party has started.

But Champagne is also a fantastic way to end a meal – i.e. at the point when cheese is often brought out. It's wonderfully refreshing and perks you up after all that food, and it's a bit unexpected, too. When given the chance, who doesn't want to round things off with Champagne?

Soft, rich cheese needs a couple of things to accompany it: texture, and something to cut through its creaminess. You could do that with crusty bread and fruity chutney, but you can also do it with Champagne. The acidity of the wine refreshes you, while the bubbles work well with the full-on creaminess of Camembert.

Because this particular kind of Champagne is made with red grapes, although the wine that you'll see in your glass is white, you still get red berry fruit flavours that will taste beautiful with your cheese, just as a chutney would. As if that weren't enough, a good Champagne will also have toasty brioche flavours – the perfect partner for cheese.

## IF YOU CAN'T FIND THIS, GO FOR…

You don't have to splash out on Champagne: as long as it's a well-made sparkling wine made in the Champagne Blanc de Noirs style, it'll work here. That could mean a wine from as far afield as England or South Africa. You could also go for a rosé Champagne/Champagne-style wine if you can't find a Blanc de Noirs.

## IF ALL ELSE FAILS, ASK FOR…

A dry, pink sparkling wine: look out for the words 'extra brut' on the label.

# Pecorino + Pecorino

### WHAT'S THE WINE?

No, that's not a misprint. Pecorino isn't just an Italian sheep's milk cheese, it's also a grape variety used to make a wonderful white wine – most commonly in the Italian regions of Tuscany, Le Marche and Abruzzo. Both grape and cheese take their name from the Italian for 'sheep' – in the case of the grapes, it's because this variety hang low on the vines where sheep can all too easily snack on them if winemakers don't take the right precautions.

### WHY THIS WINE?

It feels like the clue's in the name, but there's more to it than that. Sheep's cheese isn't generally as high in fat as cow's milk cheese, so there's no need for a wine with huge amounts of acidity to cut through the fat. What you do get in this kind of classic Italian hard sheep's cheese are more delicate but definite salty, umami flavours, perhaps with a subtle hint of minerality. You don't want to overpower those flavours, so a wine with Pecorino's gentle fruit and stone fruit flavours will be ideal.

This is one of the few wines – although it sounds mad – that really, actually tastes of grapes, and fresh green grapes at that. So imagine a bunch of bright juicy grapes on the cheeseboard next to your Pecorino, then drink their flavours instead.

### IF YOU CAN'T FIND THIS, GO FOR...

Other Italian whites from the same regions of Tuscany, Le Marche and Abruzzo: look for grapes including Trebbiano and Verdicchio. A well-made (not entry-level price) Pinot Grigio with some fruit will also work.

### IF ALL ELSE FAILS, ASK FOR...

An Italian white with some complexity and nutty notes if possible. 'Waxy' is a word that's sometimes used to describe certain white wines, and is a good tasting note to look out for here.

# Parmigiano-Reggiano + Franciacorta

## WHAT'S THE WINE?

A white, sparkling Italian wine: no, not Prosecco. Franciacorta is made in the Lombardy region from the same grapes used to make Champagne. Franciacorta is also produced in a way that has far more in common with Champagne than Prosecco, so it's no surprise that it tastes closer to Champagne than to Prosecco, too.

## WHY THIS WINE?

Parmesan – or Parmigiano-Reggiano, as the 'official' and best versions of this style of cheese are called, according to the same laws that govern the names of many wines – is more often added to a dish than eaten on its own. But that's changing, and rightfully so, because high-quality Parmigiano-Reggiano is up there with the best cheeses in the world and is well worth savouring by the sliver (or the chunk). It's intensely flavoured and deliciously salty, so it needs to be served with something that can mellow it out as well as intensify its nutty characteristics.

Franciacorta is incredibly refreshing because, well, bubbles – but thanks to the way it's aged, it also has nutty, toasty flavours that really complement the cheese. Parmigiano-Reggiano is great with dried fruits, and this wine will fill your mouth with the flavours of dried apricots. (This is one of the ways in which you can tell Franciacorta from Champagne – the warmer Italian climate gives the 'Italian Champagne' riper stone fruit flavours than its French cousin.)

## IF YOU CAN'T FIND THIS, GO FOR…

An MCC – that is, 'Méthode Cap Classique' – sparkling white from South Africa; a sparkling white from California; or any dry sparkling wine labelled 'champagne method' (or méthode champenoise) – which tells you it was made in the same way as Champagne and Franciacorta.

## IF ALL ELSE FAILS, ASK FOR…

A dry, complex, sparkling white wine.

# Aged Cheddar + Chilean Cabernet Sauvignon

WHAT'S THE WINE?

A red wine made in Chile from the Cabernet Sauvignon grape. This is Chile's most widely grown grape and the country has become masterly at turning it into excellent but affordable wines. The Maipo region arguably produces the best Cabernet Sauvignon in Chile.

These wines have brilliantly balanced acidity and tannins, and some are good enough that they can be aged for many years. But don't worry about that when you're shopping: look for a wine that's at its best right now.

WHY THIS WINE?

It feels fitting to drink what must be the world's most popular cheese with wine made from the world's most popular grape. Mature Cheddar (or any of the thousands of Cheddar-style cheeses made all over the world) isn't as salty as some hard cheeses like Parmesan, so a dry wine is called for, but with enough acidity to be refreshing.

A good experiment here is to take a sip of the wine before you have a bite of cheese, then sip again: you'll notice the wine tastes and feels much softer. That's the protein in the cheese interacting with the tannins in the wine.

IF YOU CAN'T FIND THIS, GO FOR...

A 'Super Tuscan' wine from Italy – that is, a wine from Tuscany made using a blend of grapes including Merlot, Cabernet Sauvignon and Syrah/Shiraz; a California Cabernet Sauvignon; or a Left Bank Bordeaux from France (look for the names of the specific areas of Margaux, Saint-Julien, Pauillac, Saint-Estèphe, Haut-Médoc and Pessac-Léognan, which make up most of the Left Bank).

IF ALL ELSE FAILS, ASK FOR...

A dry, bold red wine with good levels of acidity and medium levels of tannins.

# Comté + Jura White

### WHAT'S THE WINE?

A white wine from France's Jura region – an Alpine land that lies east of Burgundy. This part of the world is the wine community's favourite little secret for incredibly interesting wines … but surely not for long.

Jura whites are mainly made from the Chardonnay grape, plus a local grape called Savagnin. But the region is perhaps best known for its unusual yellow wines, whose colour and flavour are created via a special production method, and you should definitely seize the chance to taste one of these wonderful wines if you get it. However, yellow wines are rare and sought-after, which means they're pricey. So for this pairing, let's assume the more classic, easily available and still delicious Jura white.

### WHY THIS WINE?

Comté is an Alpine cheese, which means this wine has been washing down this cheese for centuries. What sets Comté apart from other cheeses is its distinctive nutty flavour – it's so special that you want a wine that can emphasise it. A white (or yellow) Jura will do just that because, along with its characteristic freshness (almost like it has captured that clear mountain air), it also has its own nutty qualities, with notes of almond. You'll perhaps get a touch of celery as you sip, too – another perfect partner for cheese.

### IF YOU CAN'T FIND THIS, GO FOR…

A dry sherry: look out for Manzanilla or Fino on the label. These varieties of sherry are both made using a method similar to that used to make yellow wine in Jura, but for a fraction of the price. Or a white Italian wine made from the Pecorino grape, which will also have a nutty character.

### IF ALL ELSE FAILS, ASK FOR…

A nutty, dry white wine, without lots of in-your-face fruitiness.

# Gorgonzola + Recioto di Soave

### WHAT'S THE WINE?

A sweet white wine from the Italian region of the Veneto, to the north of Venice. 'Recioto' refers to the particular sweet style, while Soave is the grape. The sweetness is obtained by drying the Soave grapes on special straw racks after they're picked, to concentrate the sugars and flavours.

### WHY THIS WINE?

Gorgonzola is both salty and sweet at once – an intensely flavoured blue cheese that can sometimes almost be too full on. A wine that can both stand up to its intensity and bring some freshness and fruit for relief is key here. That's why in Italy Gorgonzola is often served with cooked pears, candied lemons and even honey.

You may wish to serve your cheese with all, any or none of the above, but either way, serving it with a glass of Recioto will do the same job for you: these wines have great acidity, for freshness, but manage to combine this with beautiful ripe fruit flavours.

### IF YOU CAN'T FIND THIS, GO FOR…

A Coteaux du Layon or a late harvest Chenin Blanc from the Loire Valley in France, a Canadian ice wine, or a late harvest Chenin Blanc or Sauvignon Blanc from the New World.

### IF ALL ELSE FAILS, ASK FOR…

A sweet white wine with good levels of acidity: look out for the words 'late harvest' on the label.

# Blue Cheese + Red (Ruby) Port

### WHAT'S THE WINE?

A sweet, fortified red wine from Porto (hence the name), in Portugal. The tradition of adding extra alcohol to wine to turn it into the port that we know today was invented by the British centuries ago to preserve the wine as it was brought over by sea, and wine-drinkers soon got a taste for it. Port is made from a huge blend of different grapes – up to 40 – and is now made in a range of styles: red, white, rosé and an aged port known as tawny. For this pairing, you want the red version, which is often called ruby port. This has a particularly fresh flavour compared with other ports.

Red port should be served slightly chilled: 30 minutes in the fridge should do it. As with all fortified wines, it will last a good while after the bottle's been opened – red port will be fine for a couple of weeks in a cool place.

### WHY THIS WINE?

Blue cheese and port is a classic pairing, but why does it work so well?

Blue cheese is deliciously, moreishly salty, and it's that saltiness which contrasts so well with the sweet, smooth wine. Think of how well a fruity chutney goes with cheese and you've got it: all the jammy fruit flavours of a red port do the same job here.

### IF YOU CAN'T FIND THIS, GO FOR…

Almost every supermarket sells red/ruby port, so you're unlikely to be too stumped. If you are, Maury is a sweet, fortified red wine from the south of France and is very similar to port. Or you could go for a big, juicy and jammy Australian Shiraz. Although these are dry wines, they can be substituted for a sweet wine here because of their rich red fruit flavours.

### IF ALL ELSE FAILS, ASK FOR…

A sweet, rich red wine, port or otherwise. Look for the words 'passito', 'recioto' or 'late harvest' on any red wines.

8

# eating out and tasting wine

# WINE FOR EATING OUT

Once you've started to think about what you're drinking with meals at home, the next time you eat out will become one more opportunity to find a dream combination. But ordering wine in restaurants can still make confident people nervous and apprehensive. It really doesn't have to: here are ten ways to get the most out of eating (and drinking) out.

**Always remember that talking to restaurant staff about wine isn't some kind of test.** It's a chance for a fruitful chat about what you like, so that you can drink something you'll love. You aren't expected to be a wine expert: nobody is, except people who do it for a living.

**You don't need to feel like you have to impress the sommelier or waiting staff.** They're the ones who should be trying to impress you. You're the paying customer, and it's the sommelier's job not just to be an expert on wine, but an expert in helping customers get something they'll love.

**Most people who work with wine do it for the love of it.** So don't feel bad about giving the staff a chance to do what they love, i.e. to help you. If you ask a wine waiter for help and engage them in their favourite subject, you'll probably make their day.

**Asking for advice from the sommelier isn't a sign of weakness, but of confidence.** Be open about what you know and don't know, and ask about anything you don't understand or recognise on the list. At the outset, it can be particularly useful to ask a sommelier how they've organised their list – by region, by grape, by style? – as everyone does this differently. Understanding their logic will help you find your way around their list more easily from the get-go.

**What you love is always a good place to start.** If it's easier to name wines you've tried and liked before, go for it – it's often the best way to describe your tastes without having to drift into wine-speak. Equally, if you've been on holiday somewhere and loved the wines you drank there, that can also be a great clue for a sommelier as to what you're into. Once you've explained what you like, be clear if you want something similar to your usual, or if you're happy to be gently led out of your comfort zone: both approaches are equally valid.

**Don't assume a sommelier is there to fleece you.** Of course, it would be disingenuous to ignore the fact that restaurants are businesses, but it's great, thoughtful service that keeps good restaurants full, not ripping off their customers at every opportunity. You don't start from the assumption (well, hopefully not) that the person who takes your food order is going to try to scam you, judge you or get you to order the most expensive dish for the sake of it, so why assume the wine waiter is, either?

Yes, wine is a lot more expensive in restaurants than it is in a shop – sometimes twice the price. But it's worth reminding yourself that spirits and cocktails have a much higher mark-up than wine in almost all instances, so if you're out and drinking, a good wine is a bargain.

**All those supposed formulae/tricks to finding the 'best value' wine on a list – pick the second-cheapest, etc – are myths.** By all means go for the second-cheapest if that's your budget, but don't think it's got some magical significance. As a general rule, you'll often get better value – i.e. the restaurant will be taking a smaller cut – on the most expensive wines, but since that means you have to buy the priciest wines to get the best deal, it's not exactly useful info if you're bargain-hunting.

**Don't be ashamed of the fact that you have a budget.** Most people need to at least keep an eye on the price when ordering wine, so you're the norm. Only oligarchs and people with big business accounts don't have to live that way. It's the sommelier's job to take your needs into account, but they can only do that if you tell them what your requirements actually are. After all, you wouldn't walk into a car dealership to buy a new ride but refuse to tell the salespeople your budget.

In fact, embrace it – be upfront about your budget from the outset. You worked hard for your money, now make it – and the sommelier – work hard for you.

You should also never be ashamed to say no if a recommendation is made that's out of your price range. In fact, it's admirable to have the confidence and self-assuredness to do so.

**Temperature is something sommeliers should be really careful about.** And yet this is something that can be overlooked. If your wine arrives too warm for your tastes, have no shame in asking them to chill it ASAP. This might even go for a red wine, as reds are often served too warm. Equally, if it's too chilly to taste at its best, ask if there's a bottle that's been stored somewhere less cold. If not, you'll have to wait – or the sommelier could decant the wine to warm it up more quickly (the decanter will probably be warmer than the bottle, which would retain its chill and so keep the wine cooler for longer).

**Make tasting the wine work for you.** Technically, when a sommelier pours you a small taste, it's your chance to check that the wine isn't faulty. However, good sommeliers will usually taste the wine to check for this before they bring it to your table, so that shouldn't happen too often. It can be hard to spot a fault unless you're familiar with a wine, but relax and let your mouth guide you: if something tastes weird or downright funky, this is your invitation to say so.

That said, it isn't always easy to spot a faulty wine from just one sip. Sometimes it takes a glass for you to become sure that there's a problem. You're still totally within your rights to flag it at this point, if so. You can also use this tasting ritual to check that the wine is at the right temperature.

There's a lot of snobbery around how you should react to this first taste. If you want to simply let the sommelier know that you're happy and that the wine is good to pour, you can tell them it's fine – and leave it at that.

But if you want to get chatting to them about the wine – and showing interest and passion is a great way to learn more, and maybe even get treated to some sneaky tastes of other wines – then this is your chance to react to what you're tasting and let them know what you think.

After all, a friend with wine is the best kind of friend, so making friends with your sommelier is one of the best moves you can possibly make.

# TASTING WINE:
# A BEGINNER'S GUIDE

There's a difference between tasting wine and drinking wine – and there's absolutely nothing wrong with just drinking it. It's good not to take wine too seriously too often and nobody wants to be that bore at a party swirling their glass and taking tiny sips when nobody else cares if the wine has high or medium levels of acidity.

But learning the basics of tasting will help you get more out of wine when it's an occasion or bottle that you really want to savour. Not only will you be in a better position to appreciate what's good in a wine, you'll be better able to spot any faults or defects that might mean you, and those you're sharing the bottle with, get less enjoyment from the wine than you should.

Tasting is something you'll get better with over time and with practice: as a beginner, you'll be impressed by how quickly you gain confidence.

## Five Simple Steps to Tasting Wine

### CHOOSE THE RIGHT GLASS.
Most of the time you don't need to worry what sort of glass you drink out of. But when you're tasting you want a glass big enough to get your nose right into, and so you can swirl the wine without spilling it everywhere. It's best to use a glass with a stem rather than a tumbler, so you can hold the glass by the stem without your hand covering up what's inside.

And avoid flutes at all costs – even if you're tasting a sparkling wine – as their narrowness prevents you from enjoying the full flavours and aromas of the wine. (In fact, you're best off avoiding flutes altogether, even when you're drinking rather than tasting, for exactly this reason.)

## POUR YOURSELF A SMALL MEASURE
You only need a couple of centimetres in the glass for tasting – any more will make life harder and possibly messier. You can top up your glass later.

## START WITH YOUR EYES
Tasting wine involves all your senses, not just taste. To get a good look at your wine, tilt your glass to a slight angle so the wine runs a little up towards the mouth of the glass. Hold it up against a white wall or other light, neutral background, somewhere that allows lots of light to shine through the wine.

You'll notice how many shades of red a red wine can be: from a bright, almost pink, berry colour, to dark, almost opaque, inky shades, to less vibrant and even slightly brown hues. White wines, too, range from almost colourless, to bright lemon yellow, to rich, dark gold. The grapes used, the vintage, the style of the wine and where it was made all affect the colour, as does age: white wines tend to darken with age, whereas reds fade and lose their vibrancy.

## GET NOSY
So much of what we think we're 'tasting', we're actually smelling, so your nose is as important as your mouth in any tasting.

Swirl the wine around the glass (the air you introduce will help the wine give off more aromas), then stick your nose into the top and take a big sniff, repeating after a few seconds.

As you smell, try to let your mind latch onto things that the wine aromas remind you of. It might be another food, like freshly cut strawberries or ground black pepper, but it could equally be something further removed, like the damp smell of autumn woods or your grandmother's powdery rose perfume. There are absolutely no wrong answers here, so let your memory run wild. Smells are so instantly evocative – as you practise, you'll become better and better at accessing and placing memories of different smells. Every time you sniff a herb, flower or piece of fruit, imagine you're building up your personal library of scents.

If the wine is faulty, you'll often pick it up via the aroma, too – look out for smells of wet dog or soggy cardboard which are signs that a wine is corked and you should send it back.

Some wines are much more aromatic than others, and some need longer to 'open up'– that is, to start to give up their aroma – after they've been poured. So if you can't smell much, you're not necessarily doing it wrong.

## GET TASTING

If you're tasting professionally, you can't afford to get drunk on the job, so you'll usually spit out wine as you go. But as you're probably not tasting dozens of wines, and it isn't your job, go ahead and swallow.

There are five elements to focus on as you sip your wine. Thinking about each in turn will help you feel your way through a wine and build up a clear idea of it in your head.

### Alcohol

Notice that lovely warming sensation in your mouth, particularly towards the back? That's the effect of alcohol, and over time you'll be able to judge roughly how strong a wine is by how it feels in your mouth. A good way to practise is to alternate a mouthful of high and low ABV wines: to find a higher ABV wine, look for one from warmer climates, such as Australia or Spain; lower ABV wines come from cooler climes, such as Austria, the Loire Valley or the UK.

### Acidity

Acidity sounds unpleasant but it's essential in moderation, balancing wine and ensuring it tastes fresh and delicious. Acidic food and drink literally make your mouth water, so concentrate on observing how much you salivate when you've had a mouthful of wine. (Try sucking on a slice of lemon to really feel this effect if you're struggling to identify it.) When you're starting out, a good way to judge acidity levels in a wine is to swill it around your mouth, swallow, then, with your mouth open, tilt your head right forward: the quicker you drool, the more acidic the wine is. As well as being a great way to judge acidity, this is also a great way to never get invited out in polite company ever again, so keep this technique for home tastings...

## Sugar

All wine has some sweetness, and acidity and sugar work to balance each other out, so some wines have high levels of both sugar and acidity. Try to set aside the experience of acidity and note how sweet the wine is as it runs over your tongue – particularly the tip, which is the part that senses sweetness most.

## Tannins

These naturally occurring chemicals create a drying, puckering feeling in your mouth. They're much more prominent in red wines than in white, and levels of tannins vary hugely between wines. While that dry feeling might sound unpleasant, higher tannin levels help wines to stand up to rich food, so are ideal for drinking alongside fattier meats or with cheese. A good compare-and-contrast exercise in tannins is to taste a wine with high tannins (for example, a Chianti or a New World Cabernet Sauvignon) alongside a wine with low tannins (try a Beaujolais). Tannins mellow and become less harsh as a wine ages.

## Length

Try to observe how long the flavour of the wine lingers in your mouth after you've swallowed it. Some wines will linger for several seconds, and the flavours might even evolve further. Top-quality wines have lots of length: compare the experience of a cheap Prosecco with a good Champagne, and the difference in length will be instantly apparent.

## Find your flavours

Much as when you smelled the wine, see if you can identify flavours that remind you of other food or ingredients. There are no wrong answers, and professional tasters pick up on everything from lychee to mushroom. Try to get as specific as you can: is that the zingy flavour of a raw apple, or the more mellow flavour of a baked apple? Is it pepper or cloves that you're reminded of? Tasting notes can be a good starting point, but whatever you taste is your truth.

# INDEX

*We'd never have done this thing without these people. Thank you…*

To our agent, cheerleader and cat-herder-in-chief, Jane Finigan at Lutyens and Rubinstein, for believing in us and making it happen at all – and to Daisy, for the introduction. To Lizzy and Lucie at Ebury, our brilliant and brilliantly patient editors. To Tegan, a legend in her own lifetime, for nailing the design. To Alice at Ebury, and to Frankie and Anna, for spreading the word. To Joe, Alex and Becks for making it all look so good.

THANKS FROM BERT…

To my Nan, who sparked my love of food. I have such fond memories of cooking in her kitchen. I'm sure cooking and baking with her put me on the right track for a career in food and drink. To my parents for all their love, support and motivation. To Beth for her honesty – and for putting up with me. To my Grandad and Gran for being so brilliant. To everyone who has helped and inspired me in my career: Lisa Harding, Mathew Rafiq-Vaz, Guy Palmer-Brown, Ali Finch, Phoebe LeMessurier, Conor Gadd, Daniel Watkins, Helen Webb, Andrew Keeling, Kevin Lynn, George Scott-Toft, Wieteke Teppema, James Comyn, Daniel Willis, Johnny Smith, Joe Parente, Frederic Grappe, Charles Pelletier, Issac McHale, Andrew Cooper-Gadd and Anne Dunn.

THANKS FROM CLAIRE…

To Mum, whose kitchen shelf of cookbooks opened up the world of food to me in the first place, and to Rupert, for putting up with us both. To Michael, my perfect pairing. To Greg, for so many great glasses together, and a real home. To Michael, Jo, Nicky, Zander and all the Les Colombières family, for the sanctuary of the most beautiful house in the world. To the bosses at my 'day jobs', first at VCCP and then at adam&eveDDB, for being not just tolerant but so supportive. And finally, to my dad – to whom, although we never got to share our lives when I was even close to being old enough to drink, I raise a glass now and always.

*Bert Blaize has worked with people and wine in some of the UK's best restaurants for 14 years.*

*Claire Strickett has worked in and around food for over a decade, as a chef, writer and marketer.*

*They met over a glass of wine. This is their first book.*

10 9 8 7 6 5 4 3 2 1

Ebury Press, an imprint of Ebury Publishing,
20 Vauxhall Bridge Road, London SW1V 2SA

Ebury Press is part of the Penguin Random House group of companies
whose addresses can be found at global.penguinrandomhouse.com

Penguin
Random House
UK

First published by Ebury Press in 2020

www.penguin.co.uk

A CIP catalogue record for this book is available from the British Library

ISBN 9781529104851

Printed and bound in Great Britain by Clays Ltd, Elcograf S.p.A.

Penguin Random House is committed to a sustainable future
for our business, our readers and our planet. This book is made
from Forest Stewardship Council® certified paper.